Copyright compliance:

practical steps to stay within the law

Copyright compliance:

practical steps to stay within the law

Paul Pedley

facet publishing

Published by Facet Publishing
7 Ridgmount Street, London WC1E 7AE
www.facetpublishing.co.uk

Facet Publishing is wholly owned by CILIP: the Chartered
Institute of Library and Information Professionals.

British Library Cataloguing in Publication Data
A catalogue record for this book is available from the British
Library.

ISBN 978-1-85604-640-4

First published 2008

Typeset from authors' disk in 10/14pt Century Schoolbook and
Franklin Gothic by Facet Publishing.
Printed and made in Great Britain by MPG Books Ltd,
Bodmin, Cornwall.

Contents

Acknowledgements

Crown copyright material is reproduced with the permission of the Controller of HMSO and the Queen's Printer for Scotland.

Disclaimer

Paul Pedley is not a lawyer and is not able to give legal advice.

Figures and tables

Figures

Tables

Legislation

Note

Throughout the book, extracts from legislation are indicated by the symbol:

and extracts from official government documentation, such as the *Gowers Review*, are indicated by:

Acts

Statutory Instruments

EU Directives and Regulations

International treaties and conventions

Case law

Abbreviations

AA	Automobile Association
ACID	Anti Copying In Design
ADR	Alternative Dispute Resolution
ALCS	Authors Licensing and Collecting Society
BBC	British Broadcasting Corporation
BHB	British Horseracing Board
BL	British Library
BPI	British Phonographic Industry
BSA	Business Software Alliance
CCC	Copyright Clearance Center
CDPA	Copyright Designs and Patents Act
CD-ROM	Compact Disc Read Only Memory
CEDR	Centre for Effective Dispute Resolution
CILIP	Chartered Institute of Library and Information Professionals
CLA	Copyright Licensing Agency
CLARCS	Copyright Licensing Agency's Rapid Clearance System
COM DOC	Commission Document
CPR	Civil Procedure Rules
CVCP	Committee of Vice Chancellors and Principals (now UUK)
DACS	Design and Artists Copyright Society
DCA	Department for Constitutional Affairs (now the Ministry of Justice)
DVD	Digital Versatile Disc
ECJ	European Court of Justice
EIR	Environmental Information Regulations
EU	European Union
FAQs	Frequently Asked Questions
FEI	Further Education Institution

FOB	Firms Out of Business
GBP	British Pound
HE	Higher Education
HEI	Higher Education Institution
HERON	(Originally stood for) Higher Education Resources on the Network
IFPI	International Federation of the Phonographic Industry
ILL	Inter Library Loan
IP	Intellectual Property
IPO	UK Intellectual Property Office
IPPR	Institute for Public Policy Research
ISBN	International Standard Book Number
ISP	Internet Service Provider
ISSN	International Standard Serial Number
JISC	Joint Information Systems Committee
LACA	Libraries and Archives Copyright Alliance
M&S	Marks & Spencer plc
MCPS	Mechanical Copyright Protection Society
NCA	National Council of Archives
NESLI	National Electronic Site Licence Initiative
NHSE	National Health Service England
NLA	Newspaper Licensing Agency
OFT	Office of Fair Trading
OJL	Official Journal 'L' Series
OPAC	Online Public Access Catalogue
OPSI	Office of Public Sector Information
OS	Ordnance Survey
OU	Open University
P2P	Peer To Peer
PDF	Portable Document Format
PNAM	Purpose, Nature, Amount and Market Impact (see Chapter 8, Section 8.3)
PR	Public Relations
PRS	Performing Right Society
PSI	Public Sector Information
RPI	Retail Prices Index
RTF	Rich Text Format

SI	Statutory Instrument
SIAA	Software and Information Industry Association
SME	Small and Medium Sized Enterprises
SOCA	Serious Organized Crime Agency
TPM	Technical Protection Measure
TSO	Trading Standards Officer
TSS	Trading Standards Services
URL	Uniform Resource Locator
USA	United States of America
USD	US Dollar
UUK	Universities UK
VAT	Value Added Tax
VLE	Virtual Learning Environment
WATCH	Writers Artists and Their Copyright Holders
WIPO	World Intellectual Property Organization

1

Introduction

This book aims to promote copyright compliance both by individuals and by organizations.

The text is divided into two main parts. First, the book considers what constitutes an infringement of copyright, and what happens when things go wrong. It reviews what the consequences might be, from a court action through to the various other forms of dispute resolution such as arbitration or mediation.

The second half of the book deals with the question of how to stay within the law, and what one can do pro-actively to minimize the risks associated with copyright infringement.

Library and information professionals take a particular interest in copyright matters, because they find themselves placed in the difficult position of on the one hand being asked by their users to provide access to content while on the other hand needing to be mindful of the legal rights of the creators and distributors of intellectual property.

For the vast majority of people, copyright is not a subject that they wish to study as an academic discipline or an area that is of interest merely for its own sake. Rather, they simply wish to be able to copy material and want to be able to do so in the knowledge and with the confidence that what they are doing is within the law.

Copyright law is extremely complex, and it feels as though you need a lawyer with you to be able to say with any degree of certainty whether copying something is allowed under the law or whether it would constitute copyright infringement.

Consulting a copy of the legislation to see what the law on copyright actually says is not as easy or as straightforward as it ought to be. While it is true that one can quickly consult a copy of the Copyright Designs and Patents Act (CDPA) 1988 on the OPSI website, it will not be of much practical use because it only shows the law as it was passed in 1988, and it does not show the law as it currently stands. The CDPA 1988 has been significantly amended over the years since it was published. It has been amended by a number of Acts, such as the Broadcasting Acts of 1990 and 1996, the Copyright, etc. and Trade Marks (Offences and Enforcement) Act 2002, the Copyright (Visually Impaired Persons) Act 2002, the Legal Deposit Libraries Act 2003, and the Government of Wales Act 2006, as well as by secondary legislation – the many statutory instruments which interpret and modify it. The Copyright and Related Rights Regulations 2003 is the most significant item of subsidiary legislation to amend the CDPA 1988.

There are a number of sources available for annotated copies of the legislation and these include *Blackstone's Statutes on Intellectual Property* and *Butterworths Intellectual Property Law Handbook* (see 'Further information' at the end of this book for details).

See also:

- unofficial consolidated version of Parts I, II and VII of the CDPA 1988, www.ipo.gov.uk/cdpact1988.pdf
- the Statute Law Database www.statutelaw.gov.uk, although the copyright legislation on the Statute Law Database has not been brought completely up to date at the time of writing.

It is also important to recognize that in England and Wales our laws are not made up solely on the basis of statute law. In addition to statute law there is also case law, which has a crucial role to play in helping us to understand how the legislation applies in a particular set of circumstances.

1.1 Copyright compliance is both a legal and an ethical issue

Respecting copyright or any other intellectual property rights is not simply a question of obeying the law. In addition to being a legal requirement, it is also an ethical issue. CILIP, the professional body for information staff, has a code of professional ethics. Entitled 'Ethical principles and code of professional practice for library and information professionals' (www.cilip.org.uk/policyadvocacy/ethics), the code states that

> The conduct of members should be characterised by . . . respect for, and understanding of, the integrity of information items and for the intellectual effort of those who created them.

It goes on to say: 'Members should . . . defend the legitimate needs and interests of information users, while upholding the moral and legal rights of the creators and distributors of intellectual property.'

In 2007 CILIP launched an Ethics website, and one of the case studies from that site is of relevance here, although there isn't currently a case study which looks directly at the ethical issues involved in copyright compliance. See: 'The subscription cheat? Is it correct to subscribe to a journal as a personal copy "donated" to the information centre, rather than pay a higher institutional subscription rate?' (www.infoethics.org.uk/CILIP/admin/index.htm, case study number 1).

1.2 Policing acts of copying

Copyright is in place largely to protect commercial interests; it is not there solely to catch people copying illegally in libraries. Information professionals are not the 'copyright police', acting on behalf of rightsholders, but they do nevertheless have to be seen to be obeying the law and not prejudicing people's livelihoods.

The Copyright Licensing Agency's (CLA's) guidance on its sticker scheme, which is designed for walk-in users of public libraries, says that

> librarians are not required to monitor private copying or police the use of the Sticker Scheme. It is for each patron at a self-service copier to decide whether or not their copying is for commercial purposes and, if so, whether to ask you for a Sticker.

There are a number of enforcement agencies and rightsholders or their representatives who may take action against copyright infringers.

The IP Crime Group, established by the UK Intellectual Property Office working in collaboration with its many partners (such as the Serious Organized Crime Agency, Assets Recovery Agency, Her Majesty's Revenue and Customs, Crown Prosecution Service, and local enforcement agencies such as trading standards organizations), produced the national IP Crime Strategy (www.ipo.gov.uk/ipcrimestrategy.pdf). The Annual Enforcement Report measures UK intellectual property crime (www.ipo.gov.uk/crime/crime-enforcement-role/crime-enforcement-report.htm).

The collective licensing societies such as the CLA and the Newspaper Licensing Agency (NLA) do act against infringers. The Copyright Licensing Agency, for example, has a Compliance Unit which investigates the unauthorized copying of books, journals and magazines by business, education and government and, where appropriate, takes legal action in conjunction with authors and publishers. Where necessary, it has been known to employ private investigators in order to verify whether the copying being undertaken is infringement.

Through its Copywatch initiative and website (www.copywatch.org), the CLA offers rewards of up to £20,000 for reliable information about illegal photocopying or scanning leading to a successful licensing outcome or to a legal action.

The narrowing of the 'fair dealing' exception from 31 October 2003 (see section 1.3 of this chapter) eliminated the vast majority of situations where commercial organizations could legitimately copy copyright materials without the rightsholder's permission or a CLA licence.

According to CLA's annual review for 2003:

> CLA's view is that those organisations which are licensed are assumed to be generally compliant, and that if they commit an infringement – unless it is blatant or on a large scale – the matter will be dealt with through dialogue and agreement. However, unlicensed organisations, especially if they have refused to take out a licence when offered, or have delayed unreasonably in doing so, are not regarded in a favourable light. CLA's Copyright Compliance Unit was established under the leadership of a former detective chief inspector of police in order to tackle the problem of consistently non-compliant organisations.

More recently, the CLA's annual review for 2007 say: 'A campaign of legal action, allied with targeted advertising and PR, successfully brought the NHS in England back to the negotiating table and in March we were delighted to announce a new agreement to restore the central licence that the NHS had previously decided not to renew.'

There are a number of other organizations which exist on behalf of right-sholders in order to protect their interests against piracy and illegal copying. These include:

- the Federation Against Software Theft (www.fast.org.uk), which was set up in 1984 by the British Computer Society copyright committee
- the Business Software Alliance (www.bsa.org), which claims to be the voice of the world's commercial software industry and to educate consumers on software management and copyright protection, cyber security, trade, e-commerce and other internet related issues
- Anti Copying In Design (www.acid.uk.com) was created in 1996 by designers to combat the growing threats of plagiarism in the design and creative industries
- Federation Against Copyright Theft (www.fact-uk.org.uk) was formed in 1984 to combat counterfeiting, piracy and misuse of its members' products.

1.3 Why is there so much legal uncertainty?

One thing which it is important to say right from the outset is that it is not possible to give black and white statements relating to copyright compliance which will apply in all circumstances. Rather, it is best to try instead to think through the process of deciding whether an act of copying is legal or not; and to highlight any areas of particular risk (see also Chapter 4, which breaks down various activities into low, medium and high risk).

It is not easy to interpret how copyright law applies in a specific set of circumstances, and there are several reasons for this.

One reason relates to the role of case law in the legal system of England and Wales. Reported cases present specific problems out of which a point of law is extracted. Formulation of the law is bottom up, from a specific event to a general principle. The point of law is known as a precedent and it is binding on other courts which are at the same or a lower level in the hierarchy. The same decision must result from another situation in which the relevant facts are the same. The law evolves by means of opinion changing as to which facts are relevant, and by novel situations arising.

Often you can only be sure that something is on the right side of the law when a judge says that it is so in court, which is a little bit late in the day. It is because there is so much legal uncertainty that copyright issues are really a matter of working out how best to minimize the risk of legal action being taken against you.

The second reason for there being so much legal uncertainty is that the key words and phrases appearing in the CDPA 1988 – the ones which make the difference between something being legal as opposed to its being illegal – are not defined; and in many cases this is quite deliberate. Undefined terms include:

- original
- substantial (and substantially)
- reasonable (and reasonably)
- fair dealing
- copying for a commercial purpose.

Original

Section 1 of the CDPA 1988 says that 'Copyright subsists[1] in original literary, dramatic, musical or artistic works'. The word 'original' is not defined in the Act, but various judges have considered the requirements of originality and they have said that for a work to be original it must be the result of the expenditure by the author of skill, judgement and experience, or labour, skill and capital.

Substantial (and substantially)

Copyright is not infringed unless the whole or a substantial part of a work has been copied (CDPA s.16(3)(a)). The problem is that 'substantial' could be qualitative as well as quantitative.

Reasonable (and reasonably)

Section 39 of the CDPA 1988, which deals with copying of published works by librarians, requires 'that no person is furnished with more than one copy of the same material or with a copy of more than a *reasonable* proportion of any work'.

While this is not set out in the legislation, the generally agreed safe copying limit for a published work is considered to be one chapter or 5% of extracts.

Fair dealing

The CDPA 1988 contains four fair dealing exceptions.[2] They are:

- fair dealing for the purposes of non-commercial research
- private study
- news reporting
- criticism or review.

The Act does not define what constitutes 'fair dealing'. It does, however, give us some pointers as to what would *not* be classed as fair dealing. With regard to fair dealing for the purposes of non-commercial research or private study, section 29(3) of the CDPA says:

Copying by a person other than the researcher or student himself is not fair dealing if in the case of a librarian, or a person acting on behalf of a librarian, he does anything which regulations under section 40 would not permit to be done under section 38 or 39 (articles or parts of published works: restriction on multiple copies of same material), or in any other case, the person doing the copying knows or has reason to believe that it will result in copies of substantially the same material being provided to more than one person at substantially the same time and for substantially the same purpose.

Section 29(4) of the CDPA says that it is not fair dealing to convert a computer program expressed in a low-level language into a version expressed in a higher-level language or incidentally, in the course of so converting the program, to copy it (these being acts permitted if done in accordance with section 50B – decompilation).

Section 29(4)(a) says that it is not fair dealing to observe, study or test the functioning of a computer program in order to determine the ideas and principles which underlie any element of the program (these acts being permitted if done in accordance with section 50BA – observing, studying and testing).

Commercial purpose

Copying for a 'commercial purpose' is not defined in the legislation. The UK Intellectual Property Office (IPO) took the view that it cannot define what is copying for a commercial purpose because it is the European Court of Justice that has the final say; and, in any case, if the IPO were to try to define it, it might well result in less flexibility for libraries and researchers.

The test is whether the research is for a commercial purpose, not whether it is done by a commercial body. The key factor is therefore the *purpose* for which the copying is done.

The law cannot expect you to do more than decide what is the case on the day you ask for the copy – this could be relevant when the commercial purpose is as yet unknown or undefined. If there is no commercial purpose on the day the copy is requested, then it would seem reasonable to sign the declaration form (see Chapter 8, section 8.4) as non-commercial.

Some research in a commercial environment could be classed as non-commercial if the purpose were entirely unconnected with the employer's commercial objectives, but such cases will be very rare.

In CDPA section 178, a section of minor definitions, the definition of 'private study' says that 'private study does not include any study which is directly or indirectly for a commercial purpose'.

For further information on what would constitute copying for a commercial purpose it is worth looking at the BL/CLA joint guidance note entitled 'Copyright Office: changes to UK copyright law' (www.bl.uk/reshelp/atyourdesk/docsupply/help/copyright/copyrightfaq/).

1.4 Terminology used in the Database Regulations

It is also worth looking at the Database Regulations (SI 1997/3032), and the key words and phrases within those regulations.

The Database Regulations introduced a new *sui generis*[3] right to prevent extraction and re-utilization of all or a substantial part of a database. According to section 3A of the CDPA 1988, the definition of a database is:

 a collection of independent works, data or other materials which –
    a)   are arranged in a systematic or methodical way and
    b)   are individually accessible by electronic or other means.

The statement that the Regulations relate to material which is accessible by electronic or other means shows that a 'database' could be either electronic or hard copy. The definition of a 'database' would encompass many websites, as well as collections of data in the form of directories, encyclopaedias, statistical databases, online collections of journals and multimedia collections.

The case of British Horseracing Board Ltd and others v William Hill Organization Ltd is all about how the Database Regulations should be interpreted. When the case reached the Court of Appeal, the judge referred a series of questions to the European Court of Justice (ECJ) (Case C-203/02) and asked for a ruling on the meaning of the key terms in the Regulations, which in turn implemented Directive 96/9/EC on the legal protection of databases.

In November 2004, the ECJ gave its judgment and interpretation of the Database Right in four cases referred to it (the cases were the BHB v William Hill case, along with three cases relating to football fixtures). The judgment conflicted with previous interpretations and also with the opinion of the Advocate General.

The necessary investment in a database is limited to that which relates to the seeking out of independent materials or data and the collection of them in a database and not to the resources used for the creation of the materials or data.

In order for infringement by means of extraction or re-utilization to occur, this must be extraction or re-utilization of a substantial part of the database; and the phrase 'substantial part' would be decided in terms of both quality and quantity.

The definitions of 'extraction' and 're-utilization'

'Extraction', in relation to any contents of a database, means the permanent or temporary transfer of those contents to another medium by any means or in any form.

'Re-utilization', in relation to any contents of a database, means making those contents available to the public by any means.

The qualitative test looks at the scale of the investment in obtaining, verifying or presenting the data and the intrinsic value of the material being extracted or re-used. The qualitative test of infringement will be much harder to pass if there is no input into or verification of the data beyond the resources used for its original creation.

The quantitive test relates to the quantity of data taken. Where only a small proportion of the whole of the database is being used, it may not be sufficient to amount to infringement on quantitative grounds. However, 'substantial' would be measured in terms of quantity or quality or a combination of both.

Repeated extraction or re-utilization of insubstantial parts of a database will not infringe unless it seriously prejudices the owner's investment in the database; and this would be likely to require the repeated taking of insubstantial parts in a way which constituted making available to the public the whole or a substantial part of the content of the database.

The European Court of Justice found that there were no ownership rights over the data or content as such, but only in the collection, verification and presentation of that content.

The judgment dramatically reduced the scope of database right protection from what people had previously thought the legislation actually meant. To receive protection under the law, the owner of a database who is also the creator of the materials collected needs to be able to demonstrate that there has been a distinct investment in the database as such, and this would be extremely difficult to prove in instances where the verification of data takes place at the time of creation.

Database creators who want to ensure that their databases are adequately protected therefore need to think very carefully about the way in which the data was created, collected and verified.

For additional information, see the ECJ press release outlining the judgment, http://curia.europa.eu/en/actu/communiques/cp04/aff/cp040089en.pdf.

Notes

1 Copyright cannot exist by itself but only within the work which has been created. It is for this reason that we say that copyright 'subsists' rather than 'exists'.

2 In the past, copyright experts referred to three types of fair dealing. I would, however, contend that there are actually four types, given that the changes to the legislation which took place in 2003 made a much clearer distinction between fair dealing for research as opposed to research for the purposes of private study.

3 'Of its own kind', with unique characteristics. Database right is a *sui generis* right because it is a right that is directed at a unique category of materials – in this case databases.

2
Copyright basics

2.1 What is copyright?

Copyright is a property right. It is designed to give legal protection to works, so that other people are not able to copy or adapt the material without permission.

Copyright is a negative right, because it is the right to *prevent* copying of work which has been created by intellectual effort.

2.2 What does copyright protect?

Section 1(1) of the CDPA 1988 sets out what copyright protects:

> **L** Copyright is a property right which subsists in accordance with this Part in the following descriptions of work –
>
> (a) original literary, dramatic, musical or artistic works,
> (b) sound recordings, films or broadcasts, and
> (c) the typographical arrangement of published editions.

Examples of types of content are given in Table 2.1.

Copyright does not protect individual names, titles, URLs, bibliographic citations, facts or headlines; although a compilation of these

Type of work	Content type
Table 2.1 Types of content covered by the CDPA 1988	
Literary works	Novels, poems and plays, newspaper articles, tables or compilations other than a database; computer programs; preparatory design material for a computer program; databases, the lyrics of a song, letters, memoranda, e-mails
Dramatic works	Choreography
Musical works	Musical compositions
Artistic works	Paintings, drawings, diagrams, photographs and sculptures; architecture; advertisements, maps, charts, plans, technical drawings, cartoons, engravings, etchings, lithographs, woodcuts, collages
Sound recordings	
Films	Videos
Broadcasts	
Typographical arrangement	

could potentially be protected by database right.

The CDPA 1988 says that 'copyright is not infringed unless the whole or a substantial part of a work is copied' (s.16(3)(a)).

2.3 Requirements for copyright

Under the CDPA 1988 copyright is an automatic protection for any work:

1 which is original
2 which is fixed in a form that could potentially be copied
3 whose creator is a British citizen, or was first published in the UK.

Original

Copyright subsists in a literary work if it is 'original'. The CDPA doesn't define the word 'original', but what we know from relevant case law is that it must be the result of the expenditure by the author of skill, judgement and experience, or labour, skill and capital, to quote phrases used by various judges in order to explain the requirement of originality.

Fixed

Copyright does not protect ideas as such, but it protects the expression of ideas or thoughts if they have been formally recorded, i.e. that are 'fixed'. For example, the idea of taking a picture of a sunset is not protected by copyright. Therefore, anyone may take such a picture. But a particular picture of a sunset taken by a photographer may be protected by copyright. In such a case, if someone else makes copies of the photographs and starts selling them without the consent of the photographer, that person would be violating the photographer's rights.

In most countries, a copyright notice is not required in order to benefit from copyright protection. This is because the Berne Convention says that the rights should be automatic, and 163 countries are signatories to the Convention. Nevertheless, if you are the copyright owner in a work it is strongly advisable to place a copyright notice on or in relation to your work, because it reminds people that the work is protected and identifies the copyright owner. Such identification helps all those who may wish to obtain prior permission to use your work. Placing a copyright notice is a very cost-effective safeguard. It requires no significant extra expense, but may end up saving costs by deterring others from copying your work, as well as facilitating the process of granting prior permission by making it easier to identify the copyright owner.

In certain jurisdictions, most notably the USA, including a valid notice means that an infringer is deemed to have known of the copyright status of the work. As a result, a court will hold that person accountable for wilful infringement, which carries a much higher penalty than for an innocent infringement.

A copyright notice generally consists of:

* the word 'copyright', or the copyright symbol ©
* the year in which the work was first published
* the name of the copyright owner.

Example: Copyright 2006, ABC Ltd

2.4 Who is the owner of copyright?

In general, the author of a work is the *first owner* of any copyright in it. Since copyright is a property right which can be bought or sold, it is important to bear in mind that the author could have assigned some or all of their rights to someone else, such as a publisher, and may not be the current owner of the rights.

In the case of commissioned works, the copyright is owned by the author. The mere fact that a work has been commissioned and paid for does not give the ownership of the copyright to the commissioning party. If you commission someone to undertake a piece of work for you, it is therefore advisable to have a written agreement in place with the person who is undertaking the work for you, in which the ownership of the intellectual property rights is covered. The agreement could assign some or all of the rights to you as the commissioning party.

For works which are created as part of employment, the copyright is owned by the employer, unless there is a written agreement to the contrary.

In order for copyright to be assigned, the assignment must be made in writing, be signed by or on behalf of the owner of the copyright, and the person making the assignment must have the necessary authority to sign the agreement.

Copyright is not a single entity, it should be viewed as a 'bundle' of rights that can be sold or granted in many different ways. The copyright owner may grant permission to a particular person or group to use a work in a certain way, in a particular format, or in a certain location, or for a certain amount of time. This point about copyright being a bundle of rights is important to recognize, because each one of the restricted acts of copying can be handled separately. Thus, for example, the copyright owner may choose to sell his or her right to copy the work in one form (say, electronic). Another example would be that of a translation. It will not just be the main author who holds the copyright, because translators will have copyright in their translations.

2.5 How long does copyright last?

Copyright duration (see Table 2.2) depends on the country of origin of the work. If the work was published in an EEA country (EU + Norway, Iceland, Liechtenstein), then the copyright in published literary, dramatic or musical works normally lasts for 70 years from the end of the

Table 2.2 Copyright duration

Category	Materials included in category	Duration of copyright protection
Literary works	Written works. Includes lyrics, tables, compilations, computer programs, letters, memoranda, e-mail and WWW pages.	Author's life plus 70 years after death. Anonymous/corporation authors: 70 years from year of publication.
Dramatic works	Plays, works of dance and mime, and also the libretti of operas.	Author's life plus 70 years after death.
Musical works	Musical scores.	Author's life plus 70 years after death.
Artistic works	Graphic works (painting, drawing, diagram, map, chart, plan, engraving, etching, lithograph, woodcut), photographs (not part of a moving film), sculpture, collage, works of architecture (buildings and models for buildings) and artistic craftsmanship (e.g. jewellery).	Author's/creator's life plus 70 years after death.
Computer-generated works	Literary, dramatic and musical works.	50 years from first creation.
Databases	Collections of independent works, data or other materials which (a) are arranged in a systematic or methodical way, or (b) are individually accessible by electronic or other means.	70 years from end of the year of death of the author, if there is one, or end of year of first publication if there is no personal author. If a database qualifies for 'database right', this lasts for 15 years, and a further substantial investment in the selection or arrangement of the contents of the database would trigger a further 15-year extension of that right.
Sound recordings	Regardless of medium or the device on which they are played.	50 years from first publication.
Films	Any medium from which a moving image may be reproduced.	70 years from the death of whoever is the last to survive from: principal director, author of dialogue, composer of film music.
Broadcasts	Transmissions via wireless telegraphy through the air (not via cable or wires), including satellite transmissions.	50 years from when broadcast first made.
Published editions	The typography and layout of a literary, dramatic or musical work.	25 years from first publication.
Crown copyright	All works made by Her Majesty or by an officer or servant of the Crown in the course of his or her duties.	Published work: 50 years from the end of the year it was first published. Unpublished work: 125 years beyond the year it was created.
Parliamentary copyright	All works made by or under the direction or control of the House of Commons or House of Lords.	Mostly 50 years beyond the year it was created.

year in which the author dies.

If a work is published anonymously, or has no personal author (e.g. company reports), then copyright expires 70 years from the first publication.

The period of protection for the typographical arrangement, that is, the printed layout of the page, is 25 years from year of publication (CDPA s.15).

Within copyright there are a series of rights:

- economic rights (see Chapter 3, section 3.2)
- moral rights (see Chapter 3 section 3.8)
- database right (a property right that subsists in a database if there has been a substantial investment in obtaining, verifying or presenting the contents of the database; it augments or strengthens copyright)
- publication right (the right to issue copies of the work to the public)
- performers' rights (the rights to perform, show or play the work in public; this would include delivery of a lecture, speech or sermon as well as a visual or acoustic presentation using a sound recording, film or broadcast)
- rental and lending right (these are rights to control the hiring or lending of a work or a copy of the work to the public).

In addition to the four main types of intellectual property (patents, trade and service marks, designs and copyright), there are also a couple of other forms of protection:

- the law of confidence, covering both confidential information and privacy; this can be used to protect trade secrets, government secrets and personal secrets
- the law of passing off.

The copyright owner may grant permission to a particular person or group to use a work in a certain way, in a particular format, or in a certain location, or for a certain amount of time.

In addition to copyright, there are also a number of 'neighbouring rights'. This is a general term taken to refer to rights outside copyright law, but related to it. It includes:

- performers' rights (rights intended to protect the performers of dramatic works, musical works, some literary works and 'variety acts' (CDPA 1988 s.180(2))
- *sui generis* database right
- public lending right.

2.6 Copyright exceptions

The CDPA 1988 contains over 50 copyright exceptions or 'permitted acts'. Where an act of copying fits within one of these exceptions, it is not necessary to get the direct permission of the copyright owner before going ahead with the copying. However, these exceptions are narrowly defined and are not intended to be some kind of 'catch all' heading under which large amounts of copying can be undertaken (see Table 2.3).

Table 2.3 Some of the main copyright exceptions

CDPA section	Exception
28A	Making of temporary copies
29(1)	Fair dealing for the purposes of research for a non-commercial purpose
29(1C)	Fair dealing for the purposes of private study
30(1)	Fair dealing with a work for the purpose of criticism or review
30(2)	Fair dealing for the purpose of reporting current events
31(1)	Incidental inclusion in an artistic work, sound recording, film or broadcast
31A	Making a single accessible copy for personal use
31B	Multiple copies for visually impaired persons
32(1)	Things done in the course of instruction or preparation for instruction
32(3)	Things done for the purposes of an examination
33	Anthologies for educational use
34	Performing, playing or showing work in course of activities of educational establishment
35	Recording by educational establishment of broadcasts [doesn't apply if there is a licensing scheme . . .]
36	Reprographic copying by educational establishments of passages from published works [doesn't apply if there is a licensing scheme . . .]
36A	Lending of copies by educational establishments
38	Copying by librarians: articles in periodicals

Continued on next page

Table 2.3 Some of the main copyright exceptions (continued from previous page)	
CDPA section	**Exception**
39	Copying by librarians: part of published works
40A	Lending of copies by libraries and archives
41	Copying by librarians: supply of copies to other libraries
42	Copying by librarians or archivists: replacement copies of works
43	Copying by librarians or archivists: certain unpublished works
44	Copy of work required to be made as condition of export
45	Parliamentary and judicial proceedings
46	Royal Commissions and statutory inquiries
47	Material open to public inspection or on official register
48	Material communicated to the crown in course of public business
49	Public records
50	Acts done under statutory authority
50A	Back up copy of a computer program
50B	Decompilation of computer programs
50C	Observing, studying and testing of computer programs
50D	Acts permitted in relation to databases [a lawful user of a database can't be prevented from doing what a lawful user is entitled to do]
51	Design documents and models
60	Abstracts of scientific or technical articles
70	Recording for purposes of time-shifting
75	Permitting recording of broadcasts for the purposes of placing them in an archive
171(3)	The public interest

Part I

Copyright infringement and what happens when things go wrong

3

What constitutes infringement, and what are its consequences?

3.1 What constitutes copyright infringement?

Copyright infringement is the unauthorized reproduction of a work which is still in copyright. Copyright is not infringed unless the whole or a substantial part of a work is copied (See CDPA 1988, s.16(3)(a)).

Since its invention the photocopier has become a common means of copyright infringement, now overtaken by digital technology, because in the electronic environment copyright works are especially vulnerable to misuse and unintended further distribution; from a technical point of view they can easily be duplicated and distributed without either the authorization of, or compensation to, the rightsholder.

One question which people ask is whether they would still be breaching copyright if they were to copy out a copyright-protected text by hand, or by typing it into a word processor. The answer is yes, that to copy the content as a sequence of words would be an infringement. What it would avoid, though, would be copyright infringement in the typographical arrangement of the work.

Copyright cannot be circumvented by selectively altering the expression of a copyright work in the process of reproducing it. In other words, copyright infringement is not limited to an exact reproduction of how the work was expressed. Infringement can also be found where there is a *substantial* taking of a copyright work.

There can be either a *primary* or a *secondary* infringement of copyright.

3.2 Primary infringement

If any of the copyright owner's economic rights are used without permission, then this is a primary infringement. The economic rights of an author are set out in section 16 of the CDPA 1988:

> (1) The owner of the copyright in a work has, in accordance with the following provisions of this Chapter, the exclusive right to do the following acts in the United Kingdom—
> (a) to copy the work (see s. 17);
> (b) to issue copies of the work to the public (see s.18);
> (b)(A) to rent or lend the work to the public (see s.18A);
> (c) to perform, show or play the work in public (see s.19);
> (d) to communicate the work to the public (see s.20);
> (e) to make an adaptation of the work or do any of the above in relation to an adaptation (see s.21).

3.3 Secondary infringement

There are also some acts which could be said to be 'secondary infringements', and these are set out in sections 22–26 of the CDPA:

- importing infringing copy (s.22)
- possessing or dealing with infringing copy (s.23)
- providing means for making infringing copies (s.24)
- permitting use of premises for infringing performance (s.25)
- providing apparatus for infringing performance (s.26).

Section 27 sets out the meaning of 'infringing copy':

> (2) An article is an infringing copy if its making constituted an infringement of the copyright in the work in question.
> (3) An article is also an infringing copy if—

(a) it has been or is proposed to be imported into the United Kingdom, and

(b) its making in the United Kingdom would have constituted an infringement of the copyright in the work in question, or a breach of an exclusive licence agreement relating to that work.

(4) Where in any proceedings the question arises whether an article is an infringing copy and it is shown—

(a) that the article is a copy of the work, and

(b) that copyright subsists in the work or has subsisted at any time, it shall be presumed until the contrary is proved that the article was made at a time when copyright subsisted in the work.

An infringement of copyright could possibly be treated as a civil or criminal offence. Copyright infringement is normally dealt with as a *civil offence* and a copyright owner can take out civil proceedings in the County Court or High Court. However, the deliberate infringement of copyright on a commercial scale may be a *criminal offence* and lead to a criminal prosecution in the Magistrate's Court.

3.4 What are the consequences of copyright infringement?

A complicated intellectual property dispute in the High Court may well cost in the order of £1 million. As a result, if the infringement is of no great financial consequence, people will tend to look to alternative ways of resolving disputes, and many cases are settled informally out-of-court.[1] These informal settlements will often be made on the basis that the rightsholder grants a licence for what is being done in exchange for either a copyright fee or a royalty arrangement. Where this happens it means that no legal precedent is set, and it may well be that the terms of the settlement are not disclosed.

The Newspaper Licensing Agency (NLA), for example, has had a number of instances in which, although it has not come to the issue of legal proceedings, nevertheless payments have been made to the NLA for unlicensed copying by a range of organizations. Indeed, the Agency used to name some of those organizations on an earlier version of its website.

The NLA has certainly brought a number of civil actions for infringement of both typographical arrangement copyright and literary copyright.

From the point of view of a rightsowner, bringing legal proceedings against an infringer is advisable only if:

1 you can prove that you own the copyright in the work
2 you can prove that infringement of your rights has taken place
3 the value of succeeding in the legal action outweighs the costs of the proceedings.

For people who are keen to know how to protect their intellectual property assets, there is a useful 'Advisory checklist on protecting IPR' in an article entitled 'Intellectual Property Rights (IPR): "Be prepared"' which appeared in the *IPR Helpdesk Bulletin* number 36, November–December 2007 – see www.ipr-helpdesk.org/newsletter/36/html/EN/IPRTDarticleN1018E. html.

3.5 Civil proceedings

The copyright owner does not have to prove that the infringer knew, believed or had reason to believe, that the work was protected by copyright, or that there was an intention to infringe the copyright; the act of infringement alone is enough. However, if infringers can satisfy the court that they were innocently ignorant and had no reasonable grounds to suspect that copyright protected the work, they may avoid orders for damages being made against them – but not orders for delivery up, or account of, profits, nor for injunctions, and certainly not for the copyright owner's legal costs of bringing civil proceedings.

Ignorance of whether a work is protected by copyright is not a defence against an infringement claim. The burden is on the user to determine whether or not he or she is acting legally. However, the criminal offences which were introduced by the Copyright and Related Rights Regulations 2003 do involve a test of *mens rea* (or knowledge), hence the use in those Regulations of words such as:

commits an offence if he knows or has reason to believe that . . .

because it is not intended to criminalize people who inadvertently do something illegal.

The majority of civil proceedings which are either threatened or which are actually started in order to stop and compensate for copyright infringements never get to the courtroom, because most infringers promptly settle with the copyright holder.

3.6 Criminal offences

Prior to the Copyright, etc. and Trade Marks (Offences and Enforcement) Act 2002, people could face up to two years in prison for wilful copyright infringement but the Copyright, etc. and Trade Marks (Offences and Enforcement) Act increased this from two to ten years.[2] Indeed, the Act ensured that the maximum penalties for wilful copyright infringement were brought into line with those already provided for wilful trade mark infringement – up to ten years in prison and/or an unlimited fine. At the time of writing (March 2008), there is an anomaly between the penalties for hard copy as opposed to online copyright infringement – and this is something which the *Gowers Review* highlighted (see Table 3.1).

Table 3.1 Penalties for online v physical infringement		
	Online infringement	**Physical infringement**
Nature of offence	Communicating to the public by electronic transmission in the course of a business or to an extent prejudicially affecting the rightsholder	Making infringing copies for sale or hire	Distributing infringing copies in course of business or to extent that prejudicially affects rightsholder, importing infringing copy into UK other than for private or domestic purposes
Summary sentence (in Magistrate's Court)	Up to 3 months in prison and/or statutory maximum fine	Up to 6 months in prison and/or statutory maximum fine	Up to 6 months in prison and/or statutory maximum fine
Sentence on indictment (in Crown Court)	Up to 2 years in prison and/or unlimited fine	Up to 10 years in prison and/or unlimited fine	Up to 10 years in prison and/or unlimited fine
Source: *Gowers Review* Table 5.3 A summary of the current penalties for online and physical copyright infringement		

The *Gowers Review* concluded that crimes committed in the online and physical environments should not be subject to different sentences and that increasing the penalties for online infringement would make the law more coherent. Recommendation 36 of the Review therefore says that the government should match penalties for online and physical copyright infringement by amending section 107 of the CDPA. It is anticipated that this recommendation will have been implemented by 2009.

The Copyright and Related Rights Regulations 2003 introduced a number of offences.

Circumvention of technological protection measures (CDPA s.296ZB)

Anyone deliberately circumventing or avoiding a technological protection measure or devising equipment to avoid it may be guilty of a criminal offence as well as a civil one. A technological measure is defined in section 296ZF as 'any technology, device or component which is designed, in the normal course of its operation, to protect a copyright work other than a computer program'. In order to qualify for legal protection a technological measure must be effective. A device is considered to be effective if use of the work is controlled by the copyright owner through either an access control or protection process such as encryption, scrambling or other transformation of the work or a copy control mechanism. It is now clearly an offence to try to interfere with such protection mechanisms or get round them to avoid the restrictions that copyright owners have attached to them.

Communicating the work to the public where this affects prejudicially the owner of the copyright

Section 107 (2A) of the CDPA says:

A person who infringes copyright in a work by communicating the work to the public -

(a) in the course of a business, or

(b) otherwise than in the course of a business to such an extent as to affect prejudicially the owner of the copyright, commits an offence if he knows or has reason to believe that, by doing so, he is infringing copyright in that work.

Infringing a performer's making available right where this affects prejudicially the owner of the copyright

Section 198 (1A) says:

 A person who infringes a performer's making available right -
  (a) in the course of a business, or
  (b) otherwise than in the course of a business to such an extent as to affect prejudicially the owner of the making available right, commits an offence if he knows or has reason to believe that, by doing so, he is infringing the making available right in the recording.

Removal or alteration of electronic rights management information is prohibited (CDPA s.296ZG)

Any attempt to interfere with electronic rights management information, remove it or retransmit a work without it is a criminal offence. 'Electronic rights management information' refers to any information which is provided by the rightsholder and identifies the work, the author or any other rightsholder, or information about the terms and conditions of use of the work, and any numbers or codes that represent such information.

3.7 Remedies

There are a number of remedies for copyright infringement and they are set out in Chapter VI of the CDPA 1988.

- A copyright owner can enforce his copyright by approaching the court for the award of damages.
- A court can also serve an injunction restricting the infringer from carrying out the infringing activity.
- An order can be passed by a court for the account of profits.
- The court can also order that the infringing goods be destroyed or delivered up to the copyright owner.

Injunction (s.96)

An aggrieved copyright owner may obtain a court order or injunction to prevent publication of a work which involves an infringement of copyright. The court would not normally allow an injunction if damages would provide a claimant with an adequate remedy.

Damages (s.97)

Damages will be awarded as far as the justice of the case may require. A court will look at all of the circumstances, but in particular at the flagrancy of the copyright infringement and also at any benefits which have accrued to the defendant by reason of the infringement

In order for an award of damages to be an effective deterrent to an infringement of copyright, infringers should not be able to keep any profits from the infringement, nor should they be able to pay any less in compensation than they would have paid had they purchased or licensed the material legitimately. Some rightsholders have suggested that the current system of damages falls some way short of the 'effective, proportionate and dissuasive' civil remedies that the EU Enforcement Directive (2004/48/EC) requires and they therefore argue that awards of damages should be increased to provide an effective and proportionate deterrent to IP infringement.

The DCMS paper *Creative Britain: new talents for the new economy*,[3] published in February 2008, says:

> Copyright infringement is a serious economic crime. It is important that the penalties available are proportionate to the harm caused to UK industries and that they act as an effective deterrent. For this reason we intend to consult on introducing exceptional summary maxima (about £5,000) in the Magistrates' Courts for offences of online and physical copyright infringement.

Recommendation 38 of the *Gowers Review* said that the Department for Constitutional Affairs (DCA) (now the Ministry of Justice) should review the issues raised in its forthcoming consultation paper on damages and seek further evidence to ensure that an effective and dissuasive system of damages exists for civil IP cases and that it is operating effectively. It should bring forward any proposals for change by the end of 2007.

In May 2007 the DCA did indeed publish a consultation paper called 'Law on damages' (CP 9/07 – www.justice.gov.uk/publications/cp0907.htm).

Question 35 asked: 'Do you agree that in the Copyright, Design and Patents Act 1988 and the Patents Act 1977 the term 'additional damages' should be replaced by "aggravated and restitutionary damages"?' And Question 36 asked: 'What are your views on how the system of damages works in relation to:

a) patents
b) designs
c) trade marks and passing off
d) copyright and related rights?'

In response to the DCA consultation, ACID (Anti Copying In Design) issued a response to the consultation paper in which it said:

> Damages under the existing legal structure are woefully inadequate and serve no purpose in dissuading those who seek criminal gain from what is still considered a 'soft crime' by continuing to make vast profits from the immoral, anti-commercial and criminal activities which they continue to pursue. Current estimates about the escalating cost of IP crime and its devastating effects on IP rightsholders would be significantly improved if there was a capability within the Court system to use aggravated and restitutionary damages as a compelling deterrent in fighting what has become a serious threat to the UK's intellectual capital, its intellectual know-how and resultant IP rights.[4]

Account of profits (s.98)

A claimant has the option to be compensated for breach of copyright either by damages or by an 'account of profits'. The account represents the profit that the defendant has made from their use of the copyright work. According to section 98(1)(c):

the amount recoverable against him by way of damages or on an account of profits shall not exceed double the amount which would have been payable by him as licensee if such a licence on those terms had been granted before the earliest infringement.

Undertaking to take licence of right in infringement proceedings (s.98)

Section 98 of the CDPA says:

 (1) If in proceedings for infringement of copyright in respect of which a licence is available as of right under section 144 (powers exercisable in consequence of report of Competition Commission) the defendant undertakes to take a licence on such terms as may be agreed or, in default of agreement, settled by the Copyright Tribunal under that section—

    (a) no injunction shall be granted against him, no order for delivery up shall be made under section 99, and the amount recoverable against him by way of damages or on an account of profits shall not exceed double the amount which would have been payable by him as licensee if such a licence on those terms had been granted before the earliest infringement.

(2) An undertaking may be given at any time before final order in the proceedings, without any admission of liability.

(3) Nothing in this section affects the remedies available in respect of an infringement committed before licences of right were available.

Surrender of infringing copies (ss.99–100)

Where a person has an infringing copy of a work in his possession, the owner of the copyright in the work can apply to the court for an order that the infringing copy or article be delivered up to him. Where an infringing copy of a work is found available for sale or hire, and for which the copyright owner would be entitled to apply under a section 99 order, then the copyright owner has the right to seize the infringing copies. However, before anything can be seized the rightsholder must give notice of the time and place of the proposed seizure to a local police station.

3.7.1 Reputation management

One might adopt the view that the risks involved in isolated cases of infringement are quite low. However, it isn't only the remedies set out in the legislation which need to be taken into account. There is also the public relations (PR) risk of being caught out for copyright infringement, because this can lead to bad publicity and harm the reputation of the organization. It should not be forgotten that in the case of quoted companies, bad publicity has the potential to affect a company's share price.

According to the Research Information Network (2006),[5] fear of the financial and reputational costs of litigation has led to barriers to effective scholarly communication in the academic community, as librarians and researchers play more than safe in their own interpretation of their rights.

3.8 Moral rights

In addition to the economic rights such as the right to copy the work, to issue copies of it to the public, or to communicate the work to the public by electronic means, the author also has four moral rights. These are:

- the right of paternity (CDPA ss.77–79)
- the right of integrity (CDPA s.80)
- the right to object to false attribution (CDPA s.84)
- the right of disclosure (CDPA s.85).

The right of paternity is the right of the author to be identified as such. This right is not infringed unless the author has asserted his/her right to be identified as the author of the work, which is why you will find at the front of most books, for example, a statement along the lines that 'Joe Bloggs asserts his right to be identified as the author of this work'.

The right of integrity is the right of the author to prevent or object to derogatory treatment of his/her work.

The right to object to false attribution is the right of persons not to have a literary, dramatic, musical or artistic work falsely attributed to them.

The right of disclosure is the right of the author to withhold certain photographs or films from publication. Under the UK Act this would apply to a person who commissions the work but decides not to have it issued to the public, exhibited or shown in public, or included in a broadcast.

Companies cannot have moral rights. For example, if the producer of a film is a company, then only the director and screenwriter will have moral rights in the film.

In some countries, such as the UK, an author or creator may waive his/her moral rights by a written agreement, whereby he/she agrees not to exercise some or all of his/her moral rights.

It is possible not only to infringe an author's economic rights, but also to infringe their moral rights. These are protected as a breach of statutory duty section103(1):

 103 Remedies for infringement of moral rights

(1) An infringement of a right conferred by Chapter IV (moral rights) is actionable as a breach of statutory duty owed to the person entitled to the right.

(2) In proceedings for infringement of the right conferred by section 80 (right to object to derogatory treatment of work) the court may, if it thinks it is an adequate remedy in the circumstances, grant an injunction on terms prohibiting the doing of any act unless a disclaimer is made, in such terms and in such manner as may be approved by the court, dissociating the author or director from the treatment of the work.

3.9 Cease and desist letters

A cease and desist letter is a threat of legal action sent by a lawyer to get you to stop doing something.

If your copyright is infringed, then you may begin by sending a cease and desist letter to the alleged infringer informing him or her of the possible existence of a conflict. It is advisable to seek the help of a lawyer to draft a letter as there are restrictions on what can be said in a cease and desist letter.

The cease and desist letter identifies specific violations of copyright or other legal provisions; demands the cessation of the infringing activity and/or other remedies; and threatens that legal action will be taken if the offending party does not comply with its terms.

A typical letter would set out:

- the details of the rightsholders' rights
- how these rights have been infringed
- what remedies they seek in order to avoid a court action
- an undertaking that you will stop the infringing activity being complained of.

In some countries, if someone has infringed your copyright on the internet, you may have the option of using what is known as a 'notice and take-down' approach:

- to send a special cease and desist letter to an internet service provider (ISP) requesting that the infringing content be removed from the website or that access to it be blocked ('notice and take-down'); or
- to notify the ISP, which in turn notifies its clients of the alleged infringement and thereby facilitates resolution of the issue.

Notes

1 See Chapter 7: 'Dispute resolution'.
2 CDPA 1988 section 107(4)
3 www.culture.gov.uk/Reference_library/Publications/ archive_2008/cepPub-new-talents.htm.
4 The full response is available from the ACID website www.acid.uk.com.
5 Research Information Network (2006) *Response to the Gowers Review of Intellectual Property*, available at www.rin.ac.uk/gowers-consultation.

4

What are low, medium and high risk activities, and how can you minimize the risks?

Chapter 1 explained how some of the key words and phrases in copyright law are not properly defined and how, as a result, it isn't possible to be sure whether a particular act of copying would constitute an infringement of copyright law.

This leads to considerable uncertainty, and as a consequence we have to think of copyright compliance as being a question of risk management.

4.1 Risk management

In order to manage the risks posed by compliance with copyright law, one needs to ask oneself:

- Does my organization make copies of other people's copyright-protected material, whether that be in hard copy or electronically?
- If so, what material is copied?
- Does the copying that is undertaken fall within one of the exceptions (library copying, fair dealing etc.); and if the answer is 'no', what is it that gives me the right to make the copies?

What copying do you undertake, and from what content?

It would be worth considering making a copyright audit. Ask the following questions:

- Do you subscribe to journals, newsletters and magazines?
- Do you get newspapers each day?
- Do you have a collection of books and reference directories?
- Do you receive e-journals or newsletters by e-mail?
- Do you have photocopiers or scanners?
- Do you or your organization make photocopies of material that is protected by copyright?
- Do you get contacts in other organizations to send you photocopies from books, magazines or newspapers?
- Do you make digital copies of material that is protected by copyright?
- Do you download whole reports and publications from the internet?
- Do you forward electronic copies of journals, articles, books or reports to multiple recipients?
- Do you download music files using peer-to-peer networks?
- Do you download software via e-mail or the internet?
- Is the same item copied many times for substantially the same purpose at substantially the same time by people working or studying together?

By what means is the copying authorized?

Once you have a clear idea about what copying is undertaken, you then need to consider whether that copying is legitimate:

- Is it authorized by one of the statutory exceptions (see the list of exceptions in Chapter 2) such as fair dealing or library privilege?
- Is it covered by a contract?
- Do you have the rightsholder's permission to copy the content; or
- Is the copying covered by a licence from one of the collective licensing societies?

Do the contracts and licences you have cover all your copying activity?

Even if you have a contract or licence in place to enable you to copy content, you still need to be clear about whether or not you are complying with the terms of the licence.

Does the licence or contract cover what you are doing in terms of:

- how many people you are sending the material to
- the status of those people (for example, are they full time employees, are they freelancers, are they clients or other contacts who are based outside the organization?)
- the location of the people the material is being sent to (do users located in overseas offices, or indeed in satellite offices based in the UK, fall into the licence's definition of 'authorized user'?)
- the purpose for which the copying is being done (for example, if there is an article in a newspaper or magazine that is quite complimentary about your company, are you allowed under the contract or licence to copy the material for use by the sales force as a sales aid?)
- whether your copying of the material constitutes republishing, for which a re-dissemination agreement would be required.

As suggested above, copyright compliance is really a question of managing risk, and it is therefore worth setting out what would be considered to be low, medium or high risk activities (see Tables 4.1–3 overleaf).

I would also add to the list of high-risk activities the copying of content by electronic means. Where rightsholders' content is available in digital form, they are much more protective of it and some will enforce their rights more aggressively. Not only that, they may well have used technological devices such as digital watermarks in order to protect their content. They want to prevent their digital content from being used, duplicated and distributed without authorization or compensation.

Imagine that you want to make a copy of a 300-page report. If the report is only available in print, think how long it would take to make the copy. How much would it cost in toner, photocopier paper, and your staff time? What would be the quality of the copy that you made? Even if you were to guillotine the photocopy and get it spiral bound, it wouldn't be anywhere

Table 4.1 Low risk copying

Activity	Risk assessment/management
Copying for users under the library regulations	Copying under library privilege is carefully prescribed in the Copyright (Librarians and Archivists) (Copying of Copyright Material) Regulations: SI 1989/1212. If your copying complies with the conditions set out in the regulations, then it can be considered to be 'low risk'. In addition to setting limits on what can be copied – (one article or a reasonable proportion) – it requires the user to sign a declaration saying: (a) I have not previously been supplied with a copy of the same material by you or any other librarian; (b) I will not use the copy except for research for a non-commercial purpose or private study and will not supply a copy of it to any other person; and (c) to the best of my knowledge no other person with whom I work or study has made or intends to make, at or about the same time as this request, a request for substantially the same material for substantially the same purpose.
One article or a reasonable amount	The agreed safe copying limits are: • one article from any one issue of a journal or periodical or • one chapter or 5% of extracts. Even these copying limits do not give you an absolute guarantee that your copying would be considered by a court to be legitimate; but sticking within these limits certainly means that the copying would be at the lower end of the risk scale.
Declaration form	When a librarian in a 'prescribed' (not-for-profit) library relies on the Library Regulations in order to copy material on behalf of a library user, the user is required to sign a copyright declaration form. In exchange, the librarian gets a statutory indemnity.

Table 4.2 Medium risk copying

Activity	Risk assessment/management
Fair dealing for research for a non-commercial purpose or private study, criticism or review, or news reporting	The fair dealing exceptions should be considered to be a medium risk, because they are not as specific as the Library Regulations. The legislation does not make it clear what would be deemed to be 'fair'. The only way that you would know for sure that your copying was fair would be if the judge said so in court. What we do know, thanks to the judgment in Hubbard v Vosper, is that fair dealing has to be judged on the basis of each individual instance of copying. Each set of circumstances will be different. Fair dealing is therefore a rather risky and unpredictable defence. Fair dealing is not a right and as such it does not provide any guarantee of immunity against an action for copyright infringement. Rather, it is a defence that you might call on if you were to be faced with an action for infringement. In such a case, you would have to prove that the copying passed the Berne 3-step test.[1]
Single copying	Making a single fair dealing copy within the agreed safe copying limits would cover copying for research which is for a non-commercial purpose or private study; but would not cover copying which was clearly for a commercial purpose. The problem is to be absolutely sure of what a court would consider to be commercial as opposed to non-commercial.

Table 4.3	High risk copying
Activity	**Risk assessment/management**
Copying whole works	It is absolutely clear from section 16(3)(a) of the CDPA 1988 that to copy a whole work would be an infringement.
Making multiple copies of the same item	Multiple copying cannot be justified if you are relying on the exceptions for fair dealing for research, fair dealing for private study, or for library privilege.
Systematic single copying	There is a repeated and systematic act when it is carried out at regular intervals, for example, weekly or monthly.
Any commercial exploitation	At the absolute top end of the scale of risks would be instances of copying undertaken without the permission of the rightsholder which lead the person who copies to benefit from that copying at the expense of the person who owns the content. You should not make money out of someone else's content, without their permission or consent, and then fail to pass any of that money to the rightsholder. A court would take into account the benefit accruing to the defendant by reason of the infringement.

near as good as the original. How easy would it be to distribute the report to multiple users? Now think about the same report as if it were available in PDF format. How long would it take to make a complete copy of the PDF? What would be the cost of doing so? Thinking about the quality of the copy, would you be able to tell the difference between the original and the copy? And how easy would it be to attach the PDF to an e-mail which could be sent out to huge numbers of people? It is precisely because of all of these things that rightsowners are nervous about their content being available in electronic formats.

In the context of library and information services, you might well provide a user with a piece of content in electronic form. You might even include a covering note which sets out very clearly that, because of copyright restrictions, it shouldn't be forwarded or further copied by the library user without their first coming back to the library so that any additional copyright clearance fees were paid. But what control do you have over the material once it has been passed to the user; and what guarantee do you have, if a file is forwarded to someone else, who in turn forwards it to someone else, that this isn't going to come to the attention of the rightsowner?

4.2 How can your business reduce the risk of infringement?

If it seems as though the copying that is taking place within your organization is at the higher end of the risk scale, you will inevitably need to think through how best to minimize those risks. It may be that you need to obtain the direct permission of the rightsholders, or that you need to investigate taking out an appropriate licence. The UK government certainly encourages the use of licensing schemes.

Litigation for copyright infringement can be an expensive affair.

- Educate the staff employed by your organization so that they are aware of the potential copyright implications of their actions.
- Mark any equipment that could be used to infringe copyright – such as photocopiers or computers – with a clear notice that it must not be used to infringe copyright.
- Obtain licence agreements or assignments of copyright where these are needed; and then ensure that staff are familiar with the scope and the limitations of those agreements.
- Prohibit staff from downloading any copyright-protected material from the internet on office computers without authorization.
- If your business makes frequent use of products which are protected by technological protection measures (TPMs), have written policies in place to ensure that employees do not circumvent the TPMs without the required authorization.
- Provide a named contact within your organization to whom people can go with any questions in order to check whether or not the copying which they intend to undertake would be permitted.

Figure 4.1 How to reduce the risks of copyright infringement

Therefore, it would be wise to implement policies that help avoid infringement.

See also Chapter 10, 'Practical steps you can take to stay within copyright law'.

Note

1   The three tests are that the copyright exception only applies in certain cases; that it does not conflict with a normal exploitation of the work or other subject matter; and that it does not unreasonably prejudice the legitimate interests of the rightsholder.

5

Some copyright legal cases and what we can learn from them

One thing which people often want to know is just how costly a copyright infringement can be. Given that so many copyright disputes are settled out-of-court, where there is no requirement to disclose the details of the financial settlement, it isn't easy to respond to such a question. However, Table 5.1 (overleaf) sets out the details of the amounts involved in the settlement of a number of important cases which have occurred since the mid-1980s. A number of these are designated below.

1984

Publishers Association v Manchester City Council

In 1984 the Publishers Association took a representative action on behalf of two publishers and two authors and all its other members following the discovery of hundreds of photocopies of a standard mathematics textbook. The author of the book was a supply teacher. One day he was sent to a school in Manchester where, on opening a cupboard to get the textbooks for the lesson, he was surprised when quantities of photocopies of his own book fell around his feet.

Outcome: Manchester City Council was ordered to pay £75,000 for the copyright infringement. The costs and publicity resulting from that case persuaded local authorities to sign up for a schools' licence with the CLA.

Table 5.1 Legal cases and their settlements

Parties	Year	Settlement
Publishers Association v Manchester City Council	1984	75,000 GBP
Copyright Licensing Agency v Dar Al Handasah	1996	50,000 GBP
Ordnance Survey Northern Ireland v Automobile Association	2001	20,000,000 GBP
Tasini v New York Times	2001	10–18,000,000 USD minus 3,500,000 USD for attorneys' fees and other administrative costs
UUK v Copyright Licensing Agency	2001	CLA was ordered to pay 25% of UUK's costs, with an immediate payment of 100,000 GBP
Sony Music Entertainment v easyInternetcafé	2003	80,000 GBP (plus 130,000 GBP in legal costs)
Lowry's Reports v Legg Mason	2003	19,700,000 USD
Hackney Borough Council v Nike	2006	300,000 GBP
SIAA v Knowledge Networks	2007	300,000 USD
Independiente v Music Trading On-line (aka CD-WOW!)	2007	41,000,000 GBP
BSA v Unnamed global media company	2007	1,700,000 GBP
McLaren (fine imposed by the World Motor Sport Council)	2007	100,000,000 USD

1991

Copyright Licensing Agency v Morgan Stanley

An overenthusiastic individual at US securities house Morgan Stanley copied a £75 book called *Warrants, Options and Convertibles* published by IFR Publishing, and then distributed one of the photocopies to a client and kept 22 copies for internal use. This infringement deeply embarrassed Morgan Stanley when it found out what had happened.

Outcome: Morgan Stanley was forced to pay an out-of-court settlement of £4030 damages. Buying the books would have cost £1725.

1994

Copyright Licensing Agency v Essenheath t/a Greenwich College

Essenheath Ltd was the trading arm of Greenwich College, an independent business college in London. The CLA acting on behalf of publishers (the Open University and Centaur Press) hired a private investigator to enrol as a student and found evidence that the college had reproduced copyright material without permission or licence for use in course work by students.

Outcome: The CLA obtained a considerable financial settlement for the unauthorized photocopying, and the college was ordered to take out a CLA licence.

American Geophysical Union v Texaco Inc.

In October 1994, over 80 publishers of scientific and technical journals brought a case against Texaco, claiming that copying by its scientists and engineers of articles from the journals for future reference constituted copyright infringement. In order to simplify the litigation, the case was limited to the specific issue of whether the copying of eight particular articles by one chemical engineer was 'fair use' under US copyright legislation. Each of the journals in question included general statements that no parts of the journal could be copied without the permission of the copyright owner. It appears that it was general practice for the library at Texaco to circulate the journals and for researchers to make personal copies of any articles which they considered useful to keep for future reference.

Even though there are differences between US and UK copyright law, this was a landmark case, which was seen as adding strength to the CLA's efforts to get companies to take out a copyright licence with them.

Outcome: a US appellate court ruled that the photocopying from scientific journals by researchers at Texaco was not 'fair use'. The court took account of the existence of a collective licensing scheme by the Copyright Clearance Center as well as the existence of document delivery services, and it concluded that corporations must either curb their photocopying or buy into licensing agreements with journals.

Texaco had proposed an out-of-court settlement under which it would pay more than $1 million to the 83 plaintiffs and purchase licences covering photocopying by its researchers.

Copyright Licensing Agency v Fournier Pharmaceuticals

Fournier Pharmaceuticals Ltd is the British affiliate of the leading French pharmaceutical company Groupe Fournier, which is one of the largest private companies in France. The company accepted that copyright had been infringed in an internal current awareness bulletin circulated to its sales and marketing staff. Publications that were cited included articles from the *British Medical Journal* and *The Lancet*.

Outcome: Fournier Pharmaceuticals Ltd reached an out-of-court settlement for copyright infringements, and agreed to take out a Business Photocopying Licence with the CLA.

1996

Copyright Licensing Agency v Store Street Press

Undercover detectives acting on the CLA's behalf investigated the Store Street Press copyshop after receiving reports of an operation to cheat authors and publishers. The CLA's investigators found huge quantities of photocopying being undertaken by the shop without either a CLA licence or the authorization of the publishers. The offending copying mainly comprised course packs (including large excerpts from works published by Cambridge University Press, Elsevier, Macmillan, Penguin and Routledge) for students at the School of Oriental and African Studies, University of London.

Outcome: The CLA exposed and stopped this photocopying scam, and the shop was liable for substantial costs and damages.

Copyright Licensing Agency v Dar Al Handasah

The CLA took Dar Al Handasah Consultants (UK) Limited – one of the largest structural engineering consultancies in the UK – to the High Court for extensive copyright infringement over a long period of time. The CLA was responding to a whistleblower who rang their Copywatch Hotline and informed them of large-scale illegal copying. The CLA then took steps to confirm the accuracy of the accusations by employing a firm of private investigators to obtain supporting evidence.

Outcome: Dar Al Handasah settled with the CLA and four of its mandating publishers for a sum of £50,000 in damages and costs. Dar Al Handasah also agreed to take out a CLA licence.

1998

Newspaper Licensing Agency v Islington Borough Council

The Newspaper Licensing Agency granted a licence to Islington Borough

Council but the Council refused to pay the NLA's invoice. When it proved impossible to resolve the matter out of court, the NLA brought a civil action for copyright infringement.

Outcome: The Council accepted an undertaking that it would not copy cuttings from newspapers in the NLA's repertoire unless licensed to do so.

2001

Newspaper Licensing Agency v Marks & Spencer plc [2001] UKHL 38 (12th July 2001)

Marks & Spencer (M&S) subscribed to a press cuttings service from the Broadcast Monitoring Company. The agency paid NLA a fee for a licence to copy the cuttings. But M&S made further copies and had no licence to make these further copies. The House of Lords ruled on whether the making of these copies infringed copyright in the typographical arrangement of the published editions of the newspaper. Often the agency rearranges the text to fit onto A4 sheets on which the cuttings are supplied.

The case went right up to the House of Lords, which ruled, on 12 July 2001, that M&S had not infringed typographical copyright by photo-copying newspaper clippings for distribution to its executives.

On the true construction of section 8(1) of the Copyright, Designs and Patents Act 1988, the words 'typographical arrangement of published editions' in section 1(1)(c) of the Act referred not to the typographical arrangement of each individual article published in a newspaper, but to the typographical arrangement of the whole newspaper. The House of Lords said that the question was therefore whether the copying amounted to a 'substantial part' of the whole newspaper.

The decision does not affect the NLA's entitlement to enforce literary copyright mandated to it. The Court of Appeal's decision in the case against M&S also makes it clear that copying of articles will not be excused by being considered to be fair dealing for the purpose of reporting news and current events, although when the case reached the House of Lords the question of fair dealing wasn't addressed.

Outcome: The litigation with M&S was settled on the basis that M&S has now taken a standard NLA licence to copy newspaper cuttings for its internal management and information purposes.

The House of Lords decision was based solely on the issue of typographical copyright. There still remains a requirement for companies to obtain a licence for the copying and circulation of newspaper articles that are protected by literary and artistic copyright.

Ordnance Survey Northern Ireland v Automobile Association

Ordnance Survey (OS) launched a High Court action against the Automobile Association (AA) in 1996 after it was caught copying dozens of OS maps. Cartographers at OS trapped the copiers by putting faults, such as tiny kinks in rivers, in dozens of maps. These helped to prove that 26 million published guides, which the AA claimed as its own work, contained straightforward copies of OS maps.

In 2000 the AA had already admitted breaching Crown copyright of 64 maps and agreed to pay £875,000 compensation. In this separate case more than 500 publications were involved with more than 300 million copies printed.

Outcome: The Automobile Association agreed to pay £20 million in compensation. The money was paid over a period of two years and covered back-dated royalties, interest, legal costs and an advance on the AA's coming royalties for the next year.

Universities UK (formerly CVCP) v Copyright Licensing Agency

Long-held UUK grudges came to a head in July 2000 during negotiations for a new licence. The CLA wanted to raise the per-student fee and also tried to introduce a separate charge for the licensing of any artwork within the material. UUK referred the case to the Copyright Tribunal, whose decisions are binding.

The Tribunal decided that over 22% of current copying is fair dealing, and took this into account in calculating the new fee. The case established that the CLA's Rapid Clearance Service (CLARCS) was both costly and complex to administer. Of the total £971,000 that CLARCS collected in 2000/01, CLA's own administrative costs on higher education copying fees alone were £355,000 – quite apart from the cost to universities.

Outcome: The Copyright Tribunal decision included a number of key rulings with regard to the CLA licence for higher education institutions:

- The photocopying fee paid to the CLA by universities per full-time equivalent student increased from £3.25 to £4.
- The Tribunal said that the new licence would operate for five years backdated to 1 August 2001, with an annual RPI uplift.
- Course pack clearances were now to be rolled into the main blanket licence.
- All artistic works are included in the licence
- The ruling made no changes to the proportion of a work that could be copied under the terms of the blanket licence (up to 5% of the total, or one chapter; one poem or one article of a work).
- Fees collected from the HE sector from July 2000 to July 2001 were not affected.
- All distance-learning students, including those overseas, are included in the blanket licence.
- CLA no longer has the power to add to the excluded categories, but can still add to the list of excluded works.
- CLA was ordered to pay 25% of UUK's costs, with an immediate payment of £100,000.

British Horseracing Board Ltd v William Hill Organization Ltd

The BHB database was being constantly updated. Indeed, the cost of continuing to obtain, verify and present the contents of the database was approximately £4 million per year, involving about 80 staff and extensive computer software and hardware. The database contained details of over a million horses. It consists of some 214 tables, containing over 20 million records. An estimated total of 800,000 new records or changes to existing records were made each year.

The BHB argued that internet bookmakers who wished to use information such as runners and riders should pay a copyright fee. While there was nothing intellectual or creative in making listings of horses, nevertheless considerable investment had gone into the creation of the lists and the Court of Appeal decided that the database was therefore protected by database right. In May 2002 it referred a number of questions concerning the interpretation of the database directive to the European Court of Justice (ECJ).

The ECJ considered the issue of whether William Hill was carrying out acts prohibited by the *sui generis* right. The Court pointed out that acts of extraction (transferring the contents of a database to another medium) and acts of re-utilization (making available to the public) of the whole or a substantial part of the contents of a database require the authorization of the maker of the database. The expression 'substantial part', in quantitative terms, refers to the volume of data extracted from the database and/or re-utilized and must be assessed in relation to the total volume of the contents of the database. In qualitative terms, it refers to the scale of the investment in the obtaining, verification or presentation of the contents extracted or re-utilized.

Outcome: The Court observed that the resources used by the BHB represent investment in the creation of the materials contained in its database. However, the verification prior to the entry of a horse on a list takes place when the data is created, and doesn't constitute investment in the verification of the contents of a database. Since the materials extracted and re-utilized by William Hill did not require investment by the BHB that was independent of the resources required for their creation, those materials do not constitute a substantial part of the contents of the BHB database.

The acts of extraction and/or re-utilization of insubstantial parts of the BHB database carried out in a repeated and systematic manner by William Hill were not held to seriously prejudice the investment made by the BHB in the creation of the database. The Court said that there is no possibility that, through the cumulative effect of its acts, William Hill might reconstitute and make available to the public the whole or a substantial part of the contents of the BHB database.

Ashdown v Telegraph Group Ltd [2001] EWCA Civ 1142

In October 1997 Paddy Ashdown, former leader of the Liberal Democrats, had made a minute of a meeting he attended with the Prime Minister and a copy of this was subsequently disclosed to the *Sunday Telegraph*. In November 1999 the newspaper published a number of articles incorporating substantial sections of the minute. The articles alleged that Prime

Minister Tony Blair had discussed with the then Liberal Democrat leader plans for a coalition cabinet.

In one of its defences of breach of copyright, the *Sunday Telegraph* had relied on the Human Rights Act provisions governing freedom of expression. However, Vice Chancellor Sir Andrew Morritt ruled in the High Court that the rights to freedom of expression did not override copyright and gave Mr Ashdown summary judgment to claim damages for breach of copyright.

Sir Andrew Morritt gave permission for the Telegraph Group to appeal. While the Court of Appeal did decide that there were certain circumstances in which the Human Rights Act could override existing copyright law, nevertheless, its ruling also went in favour of Mr Ashdown. The Court of Appeal judgment clarifies that the courts will allow unauthorized use of copyright works under either the fair dealing defence or section 171(3) public interest exemption, provided that the copying is limited to what is required to serve the public interest rather than the commercial interests of the publisher.

Outcome: Telegraph Group Limited was ordered to pay 95% of Paddy Ashdown's costs; and to pay £20,000 on account of costs into court within 14 days. Leave to appeal to the House of Lords was refused.

Tasini v New York Times 533 U.S. 483

This is a landmark lawsuit which was brought by members of the National Writers Union against The New York Times Company, Newsday Inc., Time Inc., LexisNexis and University Microfilms Inc., charging copyright violation regarding the electronic re-use of work produced and sold on a freelance basis.

For many years freelance writers sold stories to American publications on the understanding that they were selling only First North American Serial Rights. These rights allowed the newspaper or magazine to publish the story in print one time only. However, with the advent of electronic media – including online databases – publishers had been selling freelance-authored material to electronic databases such as LexisNexis, even though the authors had not assigned copyright in their electronic rights and without any additional payment being made to the original authors.

Outcome: The judges ruled that, even when there is no contract relating to electronic rights, a print publisher may not put the writings of free-lancers on databases and CD-ROMs that include the entire textual content of the print publication. In effect, unless there is a written contract to the contrary, freelancers automatically retain electronic rights to their printed work.

The freelance writers had wanted payment for their work being made available on the online hosts. However, what happened instead was that the hosts removed many articles from their services.

The financial settlement was between $10 million and $18 million minus $3.5 million for attorneys' fees and other administrative costs.

From the publishers' point of view, it is imperative that they get their freelance writers to sign copyright assignment forms; and – just as importantly – that they take good care of those assignments, and are able to produce them if they are ever challenged by a freelancer who claims that they have never handed over their electronic rights.

From the point of view of people who have signed an agreement with an online service, they need to ensure that their agreements contain a warranty which confirms that the licensor has the legal right to licence use of the copyright material, and that it does not infringe the intellectual property rights of any third party; and the warranty should also be backed up by an indemnity to this effect.

2002

Copyright Licensing Agency v Photocopier Maintenance and Servicing

Photocopier Maintenance and Servicing, a private copyshop in Nottingham, was copying entire books in the fields of medicine, law, business management, marketing and computers, which were then being offered for sale to local students for a fraction of the price it would have cost them to purchase the actual publications.

Outcome: Following a covert investigation, the CLA acting on behalf of its authors and publishers obtained a High Court injunction. The CLA and its lawyers, Denton Wilde Sapte, entered the premises and enforced the order. Over 500 copies of some 100 titles were seized. The proprietor agreed to a consent order giving undertakings to the Court regarding future illegal copying: any breach of the court undertakings could result in a fine, imprisonment or seizure of assets. The proprietor also agreed to take out a CLA licence and to pay an undisclosed sum in costs and damages.

Kelly v Arriba Soft Corporation

The case Kelly v Arriba Soft Corporation involved a 'visual search engine' located at www.ditto.com. Ditto (formerly known as Arriba) trawls the web to produce 'thumbnail' images of millions of photographs, including those of Les Kelly, a photographer of the American West, who sued it for reproducing miniatures of his images without his permission and using them to link to his original photos.

Arriba Soft operates a search engine that displays its results in the form of small pictures (thumbnails) and a user may also view a larger version of the same picture within the context of Arriba's website. Arriba obtained its thumbnail images by copying images from other websites. The larger versions were imported directly from the plaintiff's website. The plaintiff Kelly sued Arriba for copyright infringement.

A three-judge panel of the appeals court rebuffed Kelly on his thumbnail claim. The court held that the use of the thumbnail pictures fell within the fair use defence because they were much smaller, low resolution images that were used for a different purpose than Kelly's works, which were artistic images used for illustrative purposes.

But in a much more far-reaching ruling, the court said Ditto could not also send users to the original photo through a link because, it argued, the use had infringed Kelly's exclusive right to display the copyrighted works publicly. It was the first time an appellate court had ruled on the issue of 'in-line linking' or 'framing', the practice followed by many search engines of providing a link that opens a browser window displaying material from another website.

2003

Lowry's Reports v Legg Mason 271 F. Supp. 2d 737

Legg Mason shared one paid $700 subscription to Lowry's Market Trend Analysis with more than 1300 employees over the company's intranet.

In mid-2003 the federal district court in Maryland found Legg Mason liable to Lowry's for breach of contract and wilful copyright infringement.

Outcome: Legg Mason was required to pay newsletter publisher Lowry's Reports $19,725,270 in damages and lost subscription fees. Legg Mason went back to court in February 2004 seeking a reduction in the award for damages; but instead the figure was upheld.

Sony Music Entertainment (UK) Limited and others v easyInternetcafé Limited (High Court, 28th January 2003) [2003] EWHC 62 (Ch)

EasyInternetcafé was found guilty of copyright infringement for allowing customers to download music from the internet onto CDs.

Background: Customers using a terminal in one of the internet cafés could download files from the internet and store them on the central server in a private directory. The private directory was cross referenced with a user ID that the customer had been given. Members of staff at the internet café were not permitted to look at the contents of the files which had been saved to the central server without the customer's permission. The customer then paid a fee of £5. This charge was made up of £2.50 for the CD and £2.50 for the copying service.

EasyInternetcafé said that it provided a significant number of warnings to customers in respect of copyright infringement. However, sections 16 and 17 of the CDPA 1988 make it clear that even if you do not know that what you are doing is unlicensed, you will still infringe any relevant copyright. Section 16(2) specifically says: 'Copyright in a work is infringed by a person who without the licence of the copyright owner does, or authorizes another to do, any of the acts restricted by the copyright.'

Even though staff at easyInternetcafé were not permitted to look at the contents of the customer's private directory without that customer's permission, the record companies had evidence of at least one occasion where staff did see precisely what was being downloaded.

EasyInternetcafé tried to defend its action using section 70 (the time-shifting principle) of the CDPA 1988, which permits consumers for private and domestic purposes to make recordings of television programmes with their video recorders in order to watch them at a more convenient time, arguing that this was what consumers were doing with music downloaded in their internet cafés. Mr Justice Peter Smith rejected the argument on the grounds that staff at the internet café were downloading the music for commercial purposes, not for private and domestic use, and that therefore section 70 did not apply.

EasyInternetcafé was found to be liable on the basis of acts being performed by its employees as part of their duties.

Outcome: In an out-of-court settlement, easyInternetcafé agreed to pay the British Phonographic Industry (BPI) £80,000 in damages for copyright infringement, plus legal costs of £130,000.

2005

London General Holdings Ltd v USP plc [2005] EWCA Civ 931

USP copied a detailed set of terms from London General Holdings for an extended warranty scheme, and produced a similar set of terms of its own. In the court case there wasn't a dispute that the document had been copied, but there was one over the calculation of how much the damages should be resulting from the infringing act.

The terms of the LGH agreement had been used to try and win some business operating a scheme of the same type as covered by the original agreement and this had resulted in a loss of income for LGH.

Copyright infringement arises from the terms themselves being copied rather than the use of the underlying idea which those terms were intended to implement. As the loss of profit in dispute arose as a result of the use of the underlying idea, rather than the actual terms themselves, the loss wasn't recoverable as damages for copyright infringement.

Outcome: Damages would be set at £35,000, which was the amount calculated on a reasonable royalty basis (or in other words, how much would have been charged for the use of those terms).

Contracts are copyright works which cannot be copied without the permission of the copyright owner.

2006

Sociedad General de Autores y Editores de España v Rafael Hoteles SA (ECJ Case C-306/05)

In answering questions referred to it by a Spanish court, the ECJ confirmed that the transmission by hotel owners of broadcasts through television sets in hotel rooms is a 'communication to the public', and could therefore constitute an infringement of copyright under Article 3(1) of the Copyright Directive (2001/29 EC). The court held that the private nature of hotel rooms did not preclude the communication of works in these rooms from being a 'communication to the public', since the test was whether a communication had been made to 'the public', not whether a communication occurred in a public or private place.

Hackney Borough Council v Nike

Nike used the copyright logo of Hackney Borough Council on a range of sportswear sold worldwide without the prior permission of the Council. In an out-of-court settlement, Nike agreed to pay Hackney Borough Council £300,000 plus legal costs.

2007

Software & Information Industry Association v Knowledge Networks

The marketing group at Knowledge Networks had been distributing 'press packets' internally to certain employees on a regular basis. These sometimes included copyrighted articles which were owned by SIAA members, even though they had been copied without authorization or licence.

Outcome: The firm reached a $300,000 agreement with the SIAA to settle the copyright infringement claims.

Independiente Ltd and others v Music Trading On-Line (HK) Ltd and others [2007] EWHC 533 (Ch) known also as the CD-WOW! case

This case involved a long-running battle between CD-WOW! and the European music industry. The legal action was spearheaded by the British Phonographic Industry (BPI) and the International Federation of the Phonographic Industry (IFPI).

The CD-WOW! website (www.cd-wow.com) is based in Hong Kong and it was selling CDs to the UK market in breach of UK IP rules on parallel importing.[1] Once ordered, the relevant products were passed by Music

Trading to the Hong Kong postal service, which then arranged their delivery to the relevant customers.

The website is hosted outside the UK; however, it is in English and is directed at customers in the UK. Indeed, Music Trading owns several UK domain names.

In March 2007 CD-WOW! was found to be in contempt of court and in breach of copyright having signed undertakings in January 2004 that it would cease to sell CDs that had first been placed on the market outside the European Union to UK and Irish customers. In addition to ruling that the company had breached an undertaking which it had given back in 2004, Judge Mr Justice Evans-Lombe ordered the company to disclose its trading records to the BPI and to pay £150,000 as a contribution to its costs.

Outcome: In 2007 the BPI was awarded £41 million in damages by the UK High Court, which was the largest settlement secured by the UK recording industry to date in a copyright infringement case (the amount was calculated by considering the cost to the music industry of the 12 million CDs that were sold illegally in the UK over the previous three years. The figure comprises £37 million to settle the BPI's 'core claim' and £4 million in interest, increasing at the rate of £9,000 a day). With UK retail sales of £21.7 million in 2005, CD-WOW! was the third-largest online retailer of music after Amazon and Play. CD-WOW! admitted in the High Court to 33 breaches of copyright law but put these down to human error. The online retailer said the fine awarded to the UK recording industry was 'excessive' and 'disproportionate' to the breaches it admitted to, and that if necessary it would take its fight all the way to the European Court of Justice.

In addition, the BPI obtained a 'freezing injunction' against the Hong Kong-based company, meaning that all of its assets are frozen (the Hong Kong office of the international law company Clifford Chance secured a 'Mareva', or 'freezing' order, to freeze CD-WOW!'s assets), which meant that CD-WOW! could fulfil orders made before the injunction was granted, but none thereafter.

Cembrit Blunn Ltd v Apex Roofing Services EWHC 111 (Ch) (5 Feb 2007)

Business letters can be protected by copyright, and to forward them to others can be an infringement.

Not every letter or e-mail will enjoy copyright protection, which is reserved for works which involve original skill or labour and which do not involve copying the work of another person. Originality in this context does not require the work to be an original or inventive thought; it only requires originality in the execution or expression of the thought. However, where existing subject matter is used by an author, independent skill must be applied to justify copyright protection for a resulting work.

Dansk Eternit Holdings wrote a letter to Cembrit Blunn, and this subsequently came into the possession of Apex Roofing. A copy of the letter had been provided to Apex by a third party, who had been given it by Cembrit in the course of a professional relationship with Cembrit. Apex alleged that this meant that the person concerned was free to circulate copies of the letter. The judge disagreed, as he felt that the letter had clearly been communicated by Apex in circumstances that imposed an obligation of confidence.

Cembrit Blunn and Dansk brought an action for breach of copyright and misuse of confidential information, claiming that Apex Roofing was not entitled to copy or circulate the letter because it was a copyright work and was confidential to Cembrit and Dansk.

The judge said that there was no doubt that it was possible for copyright to subsist in business correspondence generally, although there might be some question about what implied licences were given with regard to the reproduction of the correspondence.

See also: 'Forwarding an email can infringe copyright', Out-law News, 14 February 2007, www.out-law.com/default.aspx?page=7768.

British Software Alliance v Unnamed global media company

In September 2007 the BSA announced that it had settled a legal dispute with an unnamed global media company concerning the use of unlicensed software. The financial settlement was for £1.7 million.

See: www.out-law.com/default.aspx?page=8477.

PennWell Publishing (UK) Limited v Nicholas Patrick Ornstein and others [2007] EWHC 1570 (QB)

Three journalists left PennWell Publishing in order to set up their own business. Their contracts prevented them from engaging in conflicting interests during employment and included a confidentiality clause, but did not prevent post-employment competition.

Ornstein had used the employer's computer to store a list of contacts. Some of the contacts he had brought with him, some he had obtained during his employment, and others had been made during his employment but not through it. He took the list with him.

The employer claimed the contacts list was its property and sought an injunction. The court agreed that anything on the computer other than purely personal information belonged to the employer, but Ornstein was entitled to copy contacts made prior to his employment and was not bound by confidentiality in respect of those.

Lessons from this case:

* A contact list contained in Outlook or some other similar programme as part of an employer's e-mail system belongs to the employer.
* Employers need a clear policy identifying ownership of information on computers.
* Had Ornstein kept his personal list separate it would have been his property.

World Motor Sport Council v McLaren

McLaren was fined $100 million by the World Motor Sport Council following accusations that it had leaked secret data from its main rival Ferrari.

The $100 million fine is 40 times larger than the previous Formula 1 record of $2.5 million.

See: www.usatoday.com/sports/motor/formula1/2007-09-13-mclaren-spying_N.htm.

Note

1   Unless you have the consent of the relevant intellectual property
    rightsowner, it is an infringement of the relevant intellectual
    property rights to supply in the European Union goods that are
    the subject of intellectual property rights and that were put on the
    market elsewhere in the world.

6

Enforcement of intellectual property rights

As the *Gowers Review* observed (p.36): 'Intellectual property rights are only useful if rightsowners are able to enforce their rights, whether on their own, through the civil courts or through law enforcement agencies such as trading standards or the police.' For that very reason there has been a focus in recent years from the EU on the enforcement of those rights. From the rightsowners' point of view, the enforcement of IP rights should in an ideal world be 'swift, affordable and judicious'; and IP crime 'must carry penalties proportionate to the harm caused and the risk of being caught'.

The *Gowers Review* (p.96) set out four criteria that are necessary for the adequate enforcement of IP rights:

1   **awareness of rights** – the public must be aware of the rights that exist and find them reasonable and acceptable;

2   **penalties for infringement** – there must be adequate sanctions to prevent would-be infringers from violating IP rights. Penalties can take the form of legal sanctions, both criminal and civil, or non-legal sanctions, such as codes of practice adopted by bodies to impose penalties on infringers;

3   **pursuit of infringers** – it is crucial that those who ignore the law and the penalties that support it, are adequately pursued by the relevant authorities; and

4 **mechanisms to resolve conflict** – once an infringer is apprehended by the relevant authority the rightsholder must have the means to enforce legal sanctions through the courts, or by some means outside of the courts.

It is important to bear in mind that copyright is essentially a private right, and that consequently the decisions about how to enforce one's rights (that is, the question of what the rightsowner does when their copyright work is used without permission) are generally for the rightsowner to take.

Where their work has been used without their permission and none of the exceptions to copyright apply, the rightsowner's copyright is said to have been infringed.

Although they do not have to, it would normally be a sensible approach for the rightsowner to try and resolve the matter with the party that they think has infringed their copyright. If they take this approach, then it will be likely to save time and money for both the rightsowner and the alleged infringer. Indeed, in some cases it may be necessary for the rightsowner to show the court that they have tried to solve the matter with the other party before starting court proceedings.

If the rightsowner is unable to resolve the matter with the other party, then going to court may be the right solution. But it would make sense to seek legal advice at an early stage, and to consider the options – what alternatives are there to going to court, such as mediation?

If the rightsowner does go to court, the courts can:

- stop the infringer making further infringing use of the material by granting an injunction
- award the copyright owner damages
- make the infringing party give up the goods to the copyright owner.

There are additional remedies available for copyright infringement on a commercial scale, which is often referred to as copyright piracy. Indeed this type of infringement would be a criminal offence. It is often linked to the wilful infringement of trade marks known as counterfeiting, where criminal offences also exist. Piracy and counterfeiting are often referred to as intellectual property (or IP) crime. (For further information on the remedies available see Chapter 3.)

So, if the infringement of the copyright work is intentional, is on a large scale and copies of the work are being made available for sale, being imported, distributed, sold or put on the internet, then the rightsowner may well feel that it would be worthwhile to inform the police or their local trading standards department.

The police or the local trading standards department can then decide whether any action, including possible prosecution, is justified. However, they are unlikely to be able to take any action at all unless the rightsowner is able to co-operate fully, including:

- providing good intelligence about the crime
- helping to identify infringing goods
- assisting with the preparation of evidence
- being prepared to appear in court and so on.

6.1 Legislation

The European Commission issued a directive – 2004/48/EC of 29 April 2004 – on the enforcement of intellectual property rights (in *OJL* 195/16 of 2 June 2004). The directive covers the enforcement of intellectual and industrial property rights, including copyright and related rights, trademarks, designs and patents. As a result of that directive, all member states are required to apply effective, dissuasive and proportionate remedies and penalties against those engaged in counterfeiting and piracy and so create a level playing field for rightsholders in the EU.

Remedies available to rightsholders in the directive include the destruction, recall or permanent removal from the market of illegal goods, as well as financial compensation, injunctions and damages. There is a right of information allowing judges to order certain persons to reveal the names and addresses of those involved in distributing the illegal goods or services, along with details of the quantities and prices involved.

The directive on the enforcement of intellectual property rights (2004/48/EC) was implemented in the UK in April 2006 as The Intellectual Property (Enforcement, etc.) Regulations 2006 [SI 2006/1028] and by changes to court rules. The directive harmonizes civil measures and procedures available for the enforcement of intellectual property rights across the European Community. For the UK the changes were minor, and much of the directive was based on UK practices.

The directive applies to all intellectual property rights, but does not include a detailed definition of intellectual property rights. There may be variations in what is covered in the various member states, but for England and Wales the most relevant definition is that included in the Court Practice Direction that sets out what may be covered by intellectual property claims. They may cover:

- patents
- registered trade marks including Community registered trade marks
- copyright and related rights
- database rights
- registered designs
- design right including Community design right
- Olympic symbols
- plant varieties
- moral rights
- unauthorized decryption rights
- hallmarks
- technical trade secrets litigation
- passing off
- geographical indications.

The directive made minor changes to the remedies available to deal with the infringement of an intellectual property right. More importantly, it ensures that consistent remedies are available across the European Community. Some additional presumptions were introduced for works subject to publication right, such that where there is a statement on a work that a named person is the owner of that work this is admissible as evidence and presumed to be correct until the contrary is proved. An equivalent presumption was also introduced for recordings of performances.

There were some minor changes to the court's power to order:

- security for damages against an alleged infringer while permitting

the infringement to continue
- that delivery of infringing goods will be carried out at the expense of the infringer
- dissemination of a judgment of the court at the infringer's expense.

The detailed implications of the directive vary across the UK because of differences in court rules, civil procedures and common law rather than in intellectual property law. For England and Wales court rules and procedures are consolidated by means of the Civil Procedure Rules (CPR), and the relevant changes for this directive are included in the 41st Update to the CPR (www.justice.gov.uk/civil/procrules_fin/contents/frontmatter/guidancenotes41preview.htm). The CPR does not apply in Northern Ireland, but equivalent changes were made there. For Scotland there are separate court rules, and differences in common law.

In addition to the enforcement directive mentioned above, there is also an amended proposal for a directive on criminal measures aimed at ensuring the enforcement of intellectual property rights (COM(2006) 168 final), and at the time of writing this hadn't passed into law, but the council debate or examination on the proposed directive was scheduled for 2008.

The Institute for Public Policy Research report *Public Innovation* which was published in 2006 makes a recommendation (p.5) that there should be better legal protections in place to ensure that consumers, librarians, archivists and commercial researchers are able to pursue non-commercial objectives without fear of recrimination.

The remedies that courts may provide to compensate for an infringement include damages, injunctions, orders to account for profits and orders to deliver infringing goods to rightsholders (see Chapter 3 for further information). The infringer may also be compelled to reveal the identity of third parties involved in the production and distribution of the infringing material and their channels of distribution. In addition, the court may order, on request, that infringing goods be destroyed without compensation.

6.2 Trading standards

In April 2007 trading standards departments were given the power and duty to enforce copyright infringement. This was as a result of the implementation of recommendation 42 of the *Gowers Review*, which says: 'Give Trading Standards the power to enforce copyright infringement by enacting section 107A of the Copyright, Designs and Patents Act 1988.'

It meant that preventing the sale of copyright-infringing goods – for example, counterfeit CDs – became one of the duties of trading standards agencies throughout the country.

The implementation of this particular Gowers recommendation was achieved through the Criminal Justice and Public Order Act 1994 (Commencement No. 14) Order 2007: SI 2007/621. It inserted sections 107A and 198A into the CDPA 1988.

These provisions complement the long-established powers and duties of trading standards officers (TSOs) under the Trade Descriptions Act 1968 and Trade Marks Act 1994 to pursue and, in England and Wales, prosecute those who sell, manufacture or distribute counterfeit and pirated goods. In Scotland prosecutions are brought by the procurator fiscal and TSOs do not have the power to prosecute these offences. Instead they will report offences to the Crown Office and in doing so they will have to comply with the Crown Office's guidance for specialist reporting agencies.

The new powers relate to the following offences under the CDPA:

- Section 107 – makes it a criminal offence to make distribute, sell or distribute in the course of business an article which infringes the copyright of another – This covers items such as: CDs, DVDs, Video, publications, books and branded products.
- Section 198 – creates similar offences for recordings – this covers pirate or 'bootleg' recordings, which infringe performers' and owner's rights.
  (Commencement of Criminal Justice and Public Order Act 1994, provisions relating to copyright, IPO, 2007, www.ipo.gov.uk/cjpo1994.pdf)

Trading standards ensure that trade is fair and lawful. Unlawful trade of pirated goods generally involves infringement of copyright, trade marks or both.

Trading standards officers are now empowered to enter premises and seize goods and documents they believe to be involved in copyright infringement. They have a general responsibility of enforcement in the area of copyright infringement, and they have the right to make test purchases, enter premises and seize goods and documents.

The Office of Fair Trading has taken on the role of championing trading standards and helping to define meaningful priorities for local authority Trading Standards Services (TSS).

6.3 Evidence required in criminal cases

In copyright-related criminal cases it is necessary to prove that the suspect knew the goods in question were counterfeit or pirate.

It is necessary therefore to prove that the defendant was making or dealing with an article in a prohibited manner and also to provide evidence as to the mental state of the person charged. This may be done by providing:

(i) Evidence that a defendant made an article for sale or hire, e.g. by showing that the defendant had possession of or access to:
- manufacturing equipment;
- blank disks;
- master copies;
- price lists.

OR

(ii) Evidence that a defendant has dealt with the article in a prohibited manner, e.g.:
- by means of test purchase;
- observation at scene;
- admissions by defendant;
- inferences from circumstances of the seizure of goods.

AND

(iii) Evidence that the activity complained about took place in the course of a business, e.g.:
- multiple copies seized;
- commercial records;
- advertisements for the goods, including those advertisements which may appear on the Internet. This may

result in the seizure of computer equipment;

- article(s) exhibited or exposed for sale on business premises.

AND

(iv) Evidence that the goods were infringing copies of copyright works:

- To obtain expert evidence enforcement officers should consult with rights owners.

AND

(v) Evidence that the copyright owner did not give permission in relation to the defendant's activity:

- To obtain expert evidence enforcement officers should consult with rights owners.

Note that in an interview a simple question such as 'Has the owner of the copyright consented?' can also provide important evidence as to consent.

AND

(vi) Evidence that either:

- the defendant knew that the goods were counterfeit; or
- a reasonable person would have known that the goods were counterfeit.

Note that suitable questioning of the defendant may provide important evidence, e.g.:

- Where did he buy the goods and from whom?
- How much did he pay for the goods?
- Does he have any paperwork relevant to the purchase of the goods?
- How can he sell the goods so cheaply?

The poor quality of the goods in question may also be relevant. If genuine goods are being sold alongside pirate or counterfeit goods, the genuine goods may also be seized as relevant evidence to underline that the defendant must have known the goods were pirate or counterfeit.

Source: www.ipo.gov.uk/cjpo1994.pdf

6.4 The role of internet service providers in tackling file sharing

Peer-to-peer applications are used to copy or distribute files, including copyrighted material such as music, films and software, without paying royalties.

Recommendation 39 of the *Gowers Report* said: 'Observe the industry agreement of protocols for sharing data between ISPs and rights holders to remove and disbar users engaged in "piracy". If this has not proved operationally successful by the end of 2007, Government should consider whether to legislate.'

For some time there have been discussions between the music industry and internet service providers (ISPs), but the talks have failed to reach an agreed solution. Key problem areas have been:

- who would arbitrate any disputed allegations?
- the number of enforcements the ISPs would be expected to initiate
- how quickly a warning e-mail would be sent out.

In January 2008 Lord Triesman, the then Parliamentary Under-Secretary for Innovation, Universities and Skills, announced that if a voluntary solution could not be reached, the government would introduce legislation.

In February 2008 the government re-iterated its intention to take action in this area when the DCMS published a white paper entitled *Creative Britain: new talents for the new economy* (www.culture.gov.uk/Reference_library/Publications/archive_2008/cepPub-new-talents.htm).

Commitment 15 in the DCMS paper says 'We will consult on legislation that would require internet service providers and rights holders to co-operate in taking action on illegal file sharing – with a view to implementing legislation by April 2009.' While a voluntary industry agreement remains the government's preferred option, nevertheless it states that it will not hesitate to legislate in this area if required; and if that proves to be necessary, it aims to implement legislation by April 2009.

Rightsowners and their representatives have certainly been lobbying hard for action to be taken. Such lobbying has been at both national and international level. The International Federation of the Phonographic Industry (IFPI), for example, has been putting pressure on regulators to require ISPs to filter the content which is carried over their networks. In its publication *Digital Music Report 2008* and an accompanying press release IFPI says that 2007 was the year that ISP responsibility started to become an accepted principle.

Filtering is, inefficient, however, and would be unable to evaluate the copyright exceptions or permitted acts (such as fair dealing for research, private study, news reporting or criticism and review).

It would seem that the additional costs of network reconfigurations would be borne by the ISPs, and therefore passed on to consumers.

Any country that creates a centralized system to monitor internet communications, and on the basis of that interception decides whose internet access will be terminated, would be creating an alarming precedent that would be vulnerable to misuse and would therefore require strong safeguards.

Such monitoring raises concerns about not only privacy issues, but also freedom of expression.

At the time of writing the government had not yet published detailed proposals on the role it will require ISPs to play in the enforcement of intellectual property rights. But it is thought that this will be based around a 'three-strikes and you are out' policy. Broadband companies who do not enforce the three-strikes system would be prosecuted, and the suspected customers' details could be made available to the courts.

Up to now ISPs have relied on their status as 'secondary publishers' who merely carry the information across their networks in order to avoid taking on legal responsibility for any infringing content. That immunity is only available so long as they are unaware of any infringing content (for example, content which is libellous, or which is an infringement of copyright). But as soon as they are made aware of it, either they have to act promptly in order to remove the infringing material or they lose that immunity. In the E-commerce Directive 2000/31/EC,[1] ISPs are treated as 'mere conduits', who are only required to remove infringing content once they have been made aware of its existence.

Kim Walker of Pinsent Masons, the international law company, says that if an ISP uses technical measures to filter and identify infringing material then they will lose the 'safe harbor' defence, because they are in effect admitting that they know they have infringing material passing across their networks. (See http://out-law.com//default.aspx?page=8868; *Government will Introduce ISP Pirate-blocking Obligation Next Week, says Leak*, 12 February 2008.)

In a ruling from the European Court of Justice, Productores de Musica de Espana (Promusicae) v Telefonica de Espana SAU, [2008] EUECJ C-275/06, 29 January 2008, the court ruled that EU law does not force the disclosure of internet users' details in file-sharing cases. Rather, it is up to each country to decide how to balance users' right to privacy on the one hand, and the copyright owner's right to protect their intellectual property on the other. Given that member states of the EU are required to have implemented in their national laws the Copyright Directive (2001/29/EC), the E-commerce Directive (2000/31/EC) and the Privacy and Electronic Communications Directive (2002/58/EC), the question arises as to whether it is possible for national laws to protect the privacy of internet users in civil cases, and this ruling from the ECJ makes clear that it is possible. But it is equally the case that, where they so wish, national laws could force the disclosure of that information in civil proceedings.

6.5 Gowers Review recommendations on enforcement

The *Gowers Review* (p.1) was asked to establish whether the UK's intellectual property system was 'fit for purpose in an era of globalisation, digitisation and increasing economic specialisation'. The answer that it came back with was a qualified 'yes'. Gowers did not think the system was in need of radical overhaul. However, 'there are three areas in which the *Review* concentrates its recommendations to improve the UK framework for innovation', and one of these relates to enforcing intellectual property rights:

- [stronger enforcement of rights] – whether through clamping down on piracy or trade in counterfeit goods – to ensure practical protection is provided for rightsowners and effective deterrents to infringement are in place;
- [lower operational costs for business] reducing costs of registering and litigating IP rights for businesses large and small – simplifying processes such as licensing and litigation, and improving education and advice; and
- [balanced and flexible rights] improving the balance and flexibility of IP rights to allow individuals, businesses and institutions to use content [information and ideas] in ways consistent with the digital

No.	Recommendation
Table 6.1 *Gowers Review* recommendations on enforcement	
35	The Patent Office should continue to raise public awareness, focussing in particular on the wider impacts of IP crime, and the exceptions to rights.
36	Match penalties for online and physical copyright infringement by amending section 107 of the CDPA by 2008.
37	Monitor success of current measures to combat unfair competition in cases relating to IP, and if changes are found to be ineffective, Government should consult on appropriate changes.
38	DCA should review the issues raised in its forthcoming consultation paper on damages and seek further evidence to ensure that an effective and dissuasive system of damages exists for civil IP cases and that it is operating effectively. It should bring forward any proposals for change by the end of 2007.
39	Observe the industry agreement of protocols for sharing data between ISPs and rights holders to remove and disbar users engaged in 'piracy'. If this has not proved operationally successful by the end of 2007, Government should consider whether to legislate.
40	DTI should consult on measures to tighten regulation of occasional sales and markets by 2007.
41	The Home Office should recognise IP crime as an area for Police action as a component of organised crime within the updated National Community Safety Plan.
42	Give Trading Standards the power to enforce copyright infringement by enacting section 107A of the CDPA 1988 by 2007.

Source: *Gowers Review*, p.8

age (*Gowers Review*, p.119). (See Table 6.1 summary.)

6.6 National IP Crime Strategy[2]

The National IP Crime Strategy is a partnership between government departments, industry and enforcement agencies, set up to determine policy on enforcing IP rights. It brings together many different organizations including trading standards, the UK Intellectual Property Office, the police and Her Majesty's Revenue and Customs (HMRC). Responsibility for its development sits with the Intellectual Property Office (IPO), which works with 12 regional groups of trading standards offices. The IPO has developed a central IP crime intelligence database, TellPat, to bring together information from industry and enforcement agencies on IP crime and the criminals involved. The *Gowers Review* supports the National IP Crime Strategy.

The Serious Organised Crime Agency (SOCA) recognizes IP crime as being linked to organized criminal activity, and devotes resources to improving the intelligence base necessary to take action. However, national policing plans do not presently recognize IP crime as a police priority as part of broader action against organized crime.

Further information

National intellectual property [IP] enforcement report 2005,
    www.ipo.gov.uk/enforcereport2005.pdf,
    www.ipo.gov.uk/annreportannex05.pdf,
    www.ipo.gov.uk/enforcereport2004.pdf.

Notes

1   Directive 2000/31/EC of the European Parliament and of the
    Council of 8 June 2000 on certain legal aspects of information
    society services, in particular electronic commerce, in the internal
    market.
2   For further information on the National IP Crime Strategy see
    www.ipo.gov.uk/crime/crime-enforcement-role.htm and
    www.ipo.gov.uk/ipcrimestrategy.pdf.

7
Dispute resolution

Where a rightsowner discovers that the copyright in their work has been infringed, if at all possible any dispute should be resolved informally. Bringing legal proceedings against an infringer is advisable only if:

- you can prove that you own the rights to the work
- you can prove that there has been an infringement of your rights
- the value of a successful legal action outweighs the costs of bringing the proceedings.

As mentioned previously, the *Gowers Review* concentrated its recommendations to improve the UK framework for innovation on three areas:

- stronger enforcement of rights
- lower operational costs for business
- balanced and flexible rights.

Under the second of these – lower operational costs for business – it considered the need to reduce the costs of litigating IP rights for businesses both large and small and simplifying the litigation process.

In its publication *Mediation of Intellectual Property Disputes* the IPO says that alternative dispute resolution would be appropriate in situations where the following apply:

- Is the cost of litigation going to be disproportionate to the disputed amount?
- Are the complexities of law, fact and relations likely to result in lengthy proceedings with a high possibility of appeals?
- Are the issues highly complex or do they involve numerous parties?
- Are the parties involved in multiple actions?
- Are the parties deadlocked in existing settlement negotiations?
- Are the parties likely to have a continuing relationship after the dispute?
- Are the issues sensitive or would they require the disclosure of sensitive information?
- Do the parties desire resolution without publicity?

(www.ipo.gov.uk/mediation.pdf)

There are a number of ways in which a dispute could be resolved, such as court, non-binding mediation or binding mediation. The choice will really depend on what you are trying to achieve. You need to ask yourself what the main objectives are that you have in mind, for example:

- If the overriding objective is to set a legal precedent, then court would be the appropriate route.
- If the main purpose is to come to a decision which is not made public, then non-binding mediation would be the best option.
- Or, if what you are looking to achieve is a rapid decision, then once again non-binding mediation would meet that objective

7.1 Court

Going to court in order to solve an intellectual property problem can be expensive, stressful and time consuming. The *Gowers Review* (p.107) recognized that '[under] the Human Rights Act 1998, a person has a right to access to the courts [. . . and] therefore rejected [the idea] of imposing incentives to mediate such as introducing mandatory mediation'.

7.2 Copyright Tribunal

The main function of the Tribunal is to decide, where the parties cannot agree between themselves, the terms and conditions of licences offered by, or licensing schemes operated by, collective licensing bodies in the area of copyright and related rights. It has the statutory task of conclusively establishing the facts of a case and of coming to a decision which is reasonable in the light of those facts. Its decisions are appealable to the High Court only on points of law. (Appeals on a point of law against decisions of the Tribunal in Scotland are to the Court of Session.)

Broadly, the Tribunal's jurisdiction is such that anyone who has unreasonably been refused a licence by a collecting society or considers the terms of a licence that is offered to them to be unreasonable may refer the matter to the Tribunal. The Tribunal also has the power to decide some matters referred to it by the Secretary of State for Culture, Media and Sport, and other matters, even though collecting societies are not involved. For example, it can settle disputes over the royalties payable to broadcasting organizations by publishers of television programme listings.

The Tribunal's jurisdiction is defined in sections 149 and 205B, and Schedule 6 of the Copyright, Designs and Patents Act 1988 (as amended).

The Tribunal is administered by a Secretary, who is a civil servant working in the UK Intellectual Property Office. It consists of a Chairman and two deputy Chairmen who are appointed by the Lord Chancellor after consultation with the Scottish Minister, and not fewer than two, but no more than eight ordinary members appointed by the Secretary of State for Innovation Universities and Skills (formerly the Secretary of State for Trade and Industry). The Tribunal operates as a panel and its members have wide expertise in business, public administration and the professions. All appointments are made for a (renewable) period of five years

The provisions covering the membership and constitution of the Tribunal are set out in sections 145 to 148 of the CDPA 1988 Act.

During the course of 2006/2007, two members of the Trade Marks Directorate at the IPO undertook a review of the Copyright Tribunal. Their recommendations and findings were published in a consultation paper[1] in the summer of 2007, and had a deadline for responses of 31 August 2007.

The consultation paper set out 30 recommendations. These included:

- The Copyright Tribunal Rules 1989 should be repealed and the proceedings of the [Tribunal] be governed instead by the CPR and practice directions.
- The emphasis should be on written rather than oral evidence.
- Expert evidence should only be allowed if strictly necessary. If there is expert evidence it should be by a single, joint expert.
- Alternative dispute resolution should be used when appropriate, [but] there should be no compulsion to use it.

It is also worth looking at the uncorrected evidence of the Innovation, Universities and Skills select committee inquiry into the Copyright Tribunal, held on 28 January 2008:

> www.publications.parliament.uk/pa/cm200708/cmselect/
> cmdius/uc245-i/uc24502.htm.

7.3 Alternative dispute resolution

Alternative dispute resolution (ADR) can be defined as: 'any type of procedure or combination of procedures voluntarily used to resolve issues in controversy. [These would] include, but are not limited to, conciliation, facilitation, mediation, early neutral evaluation, adjudication, arbitration and the use of ombudsmen' (*Gowers Review*, p.106).

In short, alternative dispute resolution is the collective term for the variety of different ways in which a civil dispute might be settled without the need for court action. This has the benefit of being much cheaper than litigation. The use of ADR 'can help to avoid the negative aspects of conflict such as damage to reputation, lost customers, and damage to company morale as well as the large cost implications'. A section of the Civil Procedure Rules (4.7) says:

> The parties should consider whether some form of alternative dispute
> resolution procedure would be more suitable than litigation, and if so,
> endeavour to agree which form to adopt. Both the Claimant and
> Defendant may be required by the Court to provide evidence that
> alternative means of resolving their dispute were considered. The Courts
> take the view that litigation should be a last resort, and that claims

should not be issued prematurely when a settlement is still actively being explored. Parties are warned that if [the protocol] is not followed then the Court must have regard to such conduct when determining costs.

(Source: Civil Procedure Rule 4/7,
www.justice.gov.uk/civil/procrules_fin/contents/
practice_directions/pd_protocol.htm)

7.4 Arbitration

Arbitration is less commonly used than mediation. It involves the use of an appointed arbitrator whose decision is both binding and enforceable. Arbitration is a much cheaper option than litigation, as it does not incur the cost of ongoing court fees. Another factor to take into account is that where confidentiality is crucial, arbitration would be an appropriate means of resolving a dispute.

Arbitration generally has the advantage of being a less formal, shorter and cheaper procedure than court proceedings, and an arbitral award is more easily enforceable internationally. It is also worth bearing in mind that with arbitration – as also with mediation – the parties retain control of the dispute resolution process.

The use of arbitration or mediation can help to preserve good business relations with another enterprise with which your organization may want to continue to collaborate or enter into a new licensing or cross-licensing arrangement in the future. It would be good practice to include arbitration or mediation clauses within licensing agreements.

7.5 Mediation

Mediation is a viable low cost alternative to litigation. It is without prejudice and confidential, unbiased and voluntary. It 'encourages swift settlement of disputes and puts the parties involved in control; and is less stressful and formal than a court' (IPO, www.ipo.gov.uk/mediation.pdf).

Mediation enables the parties to devise solutions which would not be possible in a litigation process, and which may be to the benefit of both/all parties, especially if there is a continuing business relationship.

Mediation involves representatives of the parties who have sufficient authority to settle the dispute. In some cases, there may be an advantage in the representatives being individuals who have not been directly involved in the events which led up to the dispute and in the dispute itself.

 There are many benefits to mediation:

- For cases which span several jurisdictions, the court of one state cannot settle the dispute on a worldwide basis. In litigation a losing party will not always give up because they lose in the first instance but will go to appeal, mediation provides a way to settle the dispute on a worldwide basis in a single procedure.
- [It] provides a swifter solution to settlement of their disputes.
- [It] makes a substantial contribution to the more efficient use of judicial resources.
- The results of a decision following on from a mediation agreement can be beneficial to the parties involved, with the so called 'win win' results of licensing or supply contracts which the courts cannot award.

(Mediation of Intellectual Property Disputes,
www.ipo.gov.uk/mediation.pdf)

Mediation involves a controlled discussion between two opposing parties. A neutral third party facilitates negotiations and in doing so assists the two parties in working towards a negotiated agreement. At all times throughout the opposing parties have the ultimate say as to whether or not they are prepared to settle their dispute, and on what terms. Mediation is a much more flexible option than litigation. It enables parties to agree a wide range of terms without being constrained by the limitations of law. Where litigation could end up with the parties being at loggerheads with one another, mediation could help to maintain positive relations between them. A High Court case could cost £1 million, whereas the costs involved in a mediation case might be of the order of £3000.

If both sides agree to mediation, the mediator will meet each side, both separately and together, in order to discuss the issues involved. Once the main issues have been identified it is then hoped that the dispute can be settled. There are no fixed results in mediation and both sides must agree on any proposed solution to the dispute. It should be borne in mind that the mediator is a facilitator. It is not they who make a decision; rather, that is down to the opposing parties. Any discussions are 'without prejudice'. They are not binding on the parties. Indeed, should they wish to do so, the parties can continue with legal proceedings if mediation fails.

As the *Gowers Review* says, the usefulness of mediation will depend on a number of different factors:

- the circumstances of the dispute
- the parties' objectives
- the engagement of the parties
- the mediator.

'Both parties have to agree to, and adhere to, the decision, taking responsibility for the decision instead of passing responsibility to a judge or arbitrator' (*Gowers Review*, p.111).

7.5.1   UK IPO mediation service

In April 2006 the UK Intellectual Property Office launched a mediation service to help companies and individuals involved in intellectual property disputes. It operates as a commercial service administered by the IPO's Search and Advisory Service. The service has a number of staff who have had training from the Centre for Effective Dispute Resolution (CEDR), and who are therefore trained and accredited mediators.

The service handles mediation requests as follows:

- A written notice is sent to the parties inviting them to consider mediation as an alternative to litigation. Litigation proceedings are stayed for 14 days for the parties to consider mediation.
- If both parties agree to mediate, litigation proceedings remain stayed until the outcome of the mediation is determined.
- Parties are able to appoint either a UK Intellectual Property Office mediator or their own mediator.
- If the parties do choose to appoint a UK IPO mediator; then all the arrangements are dealt with by the Search and Advisory Service.
- Litigation proceedings will recommence if no mediation settlement is reached or the parties do not agree to mediate.

The UK Intellectual Property Office mediation service covers all types of intellectual property rights. This includes the unregistered copyright and design rights, as well as the registered rights such as patents, trademarks and registered designs.

There is no obligation to use UK Intellectual Property Office mediators, indeed the UK Intellectual Property Office makes available a list of other mediation providers. If people choose the UK Intellectual Property Office mediator, they will deal with the arrangements for mediation, which include issuing written notices and handling fees, and will issue a mediation agreement, which both parties will have to sign in order to confirm that they agree to:

- use mediation to try and resolve their dispute
- use a mediator provided or suggested by the UK Intellectual Property Office
- the location and costs associated with the mediation.

The costs (at the time of writing – March 2008) for one of the UK Intellectual Property Office's mediators, including accommodation for the mediation, general administration and travelling expenses, are:

Venue	Full day (GBP)	Half day (GBP)
Central London	£1000	£750
Newport	£750	£500

Another option available is for accommodation only. The UK Intellectual Property Office has suitable accommodation available for the parties to mediate at their London or Newport offices, and under the 'accommodation only' option these facilities are available when other mediators are selected to handle IP disputes. The cost for accommodation at either location is £100 plus VAT per half day. In addition, users of this facility would need to agree the fees for employing an alternative mediator to the UK Intellectual Property Office mediator. When using the UK Intellectual Property Office mediator there is no separate accommodation charge because this is included within the price.

All costs are subject to VAT for UK customers and will be borne equally by the parties unless agreed otherwise.

The World Intellectual Property Organization (WIPO) also has ADR procedures of mediation and arbitration, where the majority of mediation cases are successfully settled.

7.6 Jurisdiction

One question which arises from time to time in relation to copyright is that of jurisdiction or applicable law. If someone were to copy an item of content, and then to email that to recipients in several countries, which law would apply – that of the country from which the copy was made, or that of the country of the recipients?

For a long time now there has been a piece of legislation in the pipeline, known as 'Rome II'. This has now been passed as a regulation, which means that it doesn't require subsidiary UK legislation for it to become law. Regulation (EC) 864/2007 of 11 July 2007 on the law applicable to non-contractual obligations (Rome II) OJL 199/45, 31/7/2007, comes into effect from 11 January 2009.

Recital 26 of the regulation says:

> Regarding infringements of intellectual property rights, the universally acknowledged principle of the lex loci protection should be preserved. For the purposes of this Regulation, the term 'intellectual property rights' should be interpreted as meaning, for instance, copyright, related rights, the sui generis right for the protection of databases and industrial property rights.

The key part of the regulation as far as copyright is concerned is Article 8:

Article 8 – Infringement of intellectual property rights
1. The law applicable to a non-contractual obligation arising from an infringement of an intellectual property right shall be the law of the country for which protection is claimed.
2. In the case of a non-contractual obligation arising from an infringement of a unitary Community intellectual property right, the law applicable shall, for any question that is not governed by the relevant Community instrument, be the law of the country in which the act of infringement was committed.
3. The law applicable under this Article may not be derogated from

by an agreement pursuant to Article 14 [in other words, where 'The parties may agree to submit non-contractual obligations to the law of their choice. . . .'].

See also Chapter 3, 'What constitutes infringement, and what are its consequences?'

Further information

Mediation of intellectual property disputes,
     www.ipo.gov.uk/mediation.pdf.
Mediation providers, www.ipo.gov.uk/mediationproviders.pdf.
UK Intellectual Property Office model mediation procedure and
     agreement, www.ipo.gov.uk/mediationmodel.pdf.
Alternatives to court: dealing with problems without going to court
     (Community Legal Service),
     www.clsdirect.org.uk/en/legalhelp/leaflet23_1.jsp.
WIPO Aribtration and Mediation Center,
     http://arbiter.wipo.int/center/index.html.
For further information on the IPO's mediation service contact:
     The UK Intellectual Property Office
     Concept House
     Cardiff Road
     Newport
     South Wales NP10 8QQ
     Tel: 01633 811010
     Fax: 01633 811020
     E-mail: mediation@ipo.gov.uk

Note

1   *Review of the Copyright Tribunal,*
     www.ipo.gov.uk/ctribunalreview.pdf.

Part 2
How to stay within copyright law

8

How to ensure that your copying is properly authorized

8.1 Is your copying authorized?

Authorization is needed for any copying of material protected by copyright or database right. However, this doesn't mean that for every act of copying you need to contact the rightsowner directly in order to get their explicit permission. There are, in fact, four main forms of authorization. These are:

- statute
- permission
- contract
- licence.

In order to be copyright compliant, you need to be clear in your own mind precisely what it is that gives you the necessary authorization to make the copy.

8.1.1   Statute

UK copyright law contains over 50 copyright exceptions. They are, however, very narrowly defined. They are certainly not intended as broad exceptions to be used in order to justify the majority of an organization's copying activity.

In the past, companies would regularly justify the copying that they did as being fair dealing for research purposes. You need to bear in mind that the fair dealing exceptions for research or private study were narrowed with the coming into force of the Copyright and Related Rights Regulations 2003: SI 2003/2498.

Whether for research or private study purposes, fair dealing does not provide the necessary permission or authorization to copy material if it is for a commercial purpose.

Another point worth mentioning is that even if the copying is for a non-commercial purpose, and you rely on the fair dealing exceptions for research or private study, you cannot rely on them to justify the making of multiple copies. Instead, they would cover only the making of single copy.

Ask yourself: 'Is the copying authorized by one of the permitted acts or copyright exceptions?' In order to answer this question you need to consider the purpose of the copying. For example, if the purpose is:

- for private study
- for research for a non-commercial purpose
- to criticize another's work
- to review another's work
- for instruction
- for examination
- for parliamentary or judicial proceedings
- for those with a visual impairment

then it *may* be authorized by one of the statutory exceptions. You would need to consider whether the copying activity that you wanted to undertake fitted within the relevant exception as set out in the CDPA 1988.

There is an exception permitting copying for instruction, for example. This particular exception is covered in section 32 of the Act, and section 32(1) makes it clear that for the copying to be permitted, it is essential that it:

(a) is done by a person giving or receiving instruction,
(b) is not done by means of a reprographic process, and
(c) is accompanied by a sufficient acknowledgement, and provided that the instruction is for a non-commercial purpose.

Given that this particular exception only applies where the copying is not done by means of a reprographic process, it is a good example of the way in which these exceptions or permitted acts are all very narrowly defined. It basically limits the copying to where one copies out the material by hand.

The reason for this is that the Berne Convention of 1886, to which 163 countries are signed up, enabled national legislatures to provide a number of copyright exceptions or permitted acts, so long as they met a three-step test as follows (Article 9(2)):

1 in certain special cases
2 does not conflict with a normal exploitation of the work [or other subject matter]
3 does not unreasonably prejudice the legitimate interests of the author.

The Copyright Directive (2001/29/EC) uses a similar form of words, and therefore any of the permitted acts or copyright exceptions appearing in the CDPA 1988 are required to fulfil the Berne three-step test.

In effect, the permitted acts or copyright exceptions make it possible for users of copyright works to undertake a limited amount of copying without having to get the permission of the copyright owner, so long as the copying is done under the conditions set out in the legislation. The permitted acts are, by definition, a lawful use of a work even though they have not been authorized by the publisher, or whoever owns the rights. They provide an invaluable counterbalance to the rightsholder's exclusive rights in the wider interests of research, scholarship and culture.

If you are sure that your copying is authorized by the exception covering copying for the purposes of research for a non-commercial purpose or private study, you will also need to ensure that the copying stays within the agreed safe copying limits,[1] which are:

- one article from any one issue of a journal or periodical
- one chapter or 5% of extracts from a book (see, for example, the CILIP copyright posters which refer to the agreed safe copying limits).[2]

Unless it is impracticable to do so, you must acknowledge all copies.

Bear in mind that this exception would not cover multiple copying; and in the case of the electronic environment that would equate to ensuring that you did not place any copy made under the exceptions for non-commercial research or private study on a shared drive or computer network.

In order to be able to say that your copying is fair or reasonable, you would really need to be able to answer 'no' to each of the questions in Figure 8.1. If you can in all honesty answer 'no' to each of them, then there shouldn't be a problem.

- Am I copying in order to profit directly or indirectly by it?
- Am I copying instead of buying it?
- Would I have bought a copy if I could not copy it?
- Am I planning to make several copies of the same item?
- Are my colleagues likely to be copying the same item for the same purpose?
- Am I damaging the integrity of the work by the way in which I am copying it?

Figure 8.1 Is your copying both fair and reasonable?

A list of some of the main copyright exceptions is provided in Table 2.3.

8.1.2   Permission

One obvious way of legitimizing any copying is to get the direct permission of the rightsholder. In order for permission to be granted you will need to provide the rightsholder with as much information as possible about what it is you want to copy and what it will be used for. The request should therefore contain the details shown in Figure 8.2.

Permissions letters or contracts must cover the scope of the content and all of the uses that you need. It is recommended that you clearly identify such things as:

- full details of the item (author, title, publication, dates, inclusive pages etc.); users; course details (for educational institutions)
- full details about requestor (institution, company, address, contact details etc.)
- full details of required permissions (to digitize, store, view, download/print etc.)

- Author and title of the extract you wish to reproduce
- Author and title of the publication in which the extract will appear
- Page range
- Publisher's name
- Date of publication (plus volume and issue numbers for journals)
- ISBN or ISSN
- Number of copies to be made
- Purpose for which the copying is being done

Figure 8.2 The details a permission request should contain

- file formats (PDF, RTF) etc.
- protection strategy and measures
- copyright policy
- other information such as the source of your digitization copy.

If you are going to be requesting copyright clearance from rightsholders on a regular basis you should consider developing a standard form for this purpose. There is an example of a standard form for permission seeking on page 73 of Sandy Norman's book *Practical Copyright for Information Professionals* (see 'Further information' at the end of this book for details).

See also Chapter 9, 'The copyright clearance process'.

8.1.3 Contract

One option to legitimize the copying is to get the permission set out in a contract. This could be a contract directly with the rightsholder, in which the copyright owner sets out how much can be copied, for what purpose, and to what audience (for example, can the content be sent to clients, or is it only for use in-house?). There are many other forms of contractual agreement in which the necessary rights can be obtained without the need to deal directly with the rightsholder.

Consortia licences

Libraries often find it useful to work collaboratively in a consortium.

Working together means that they are able to negotiate good deals with the suppliers because of their collective buying power. Licence negotiations can be time consuming, and another key reason for libraries to form consortia is because this doesn't require each institution or organization to negotiate separately with the publisher. The negotiation team working for the consortium is able to build up considerable expertise in this specialized area.

One example of a consortia agreement is NESLi2 (www.nesli2.ac.uk), the UK's national initiative for the licensing of electronic journals on behalf of the higher and further education and research communities. NESLi2 is a product of the JISC and underwritten by the Higher Education Funding Council for England on behalf of the funding bodies. Key features of NESLi2 are:

- use of the Model NESLi2 Licence for Journals
- a clearly defined list of publishers to seek agreements with, based on feedback from the community
- an independent and experienced negotiation agent
- pre-defined criteria to assist the negotiation process
- flexible order channels and access routes.

Shrink wrap

Neither a shrink-wrap nor a click-use licence is negotiable. If you receive an item such as a book or CD-ROM encased in plastic and there is a set of licence terms clearly visible, you will be bound by the terms of the agreement if you go ahead and open the item.

Click-use licence

These are licences which are set out in a format in which you are required to click a button where you are agreeing to a set of terms and conditions. This happens when you install many software packages, and they are also used on a number of websites which won't allow you beyond the licence page until you have agreed to the website's terms and conditions. Some licence agreements are set out in a way that requires the user to scroll down the terms of the agreement in order to be able to click 'Yes' or 'I agree', even where you are happy to sign up to the terms.

There is no opportunity to negotiate the licence terms, and you can only gain access to the website or load the product if you click on something along the lines of an 'I ACCEPT' the terms and conditions, positively confirming that you are agreeing to the terms.

Crown and parliamentary copyright waiver

The White Paper *The Future Management of Crown Copyright* (Cm 4300), which was issued on 26 March 1999, announced a new policy on Crown copyright which allowed for unrestricted copying and reproduction of certain categories of Crown copyright material.

Some Crown copyright material is thus now covered by waiver conditions. This covers material where copyright is asserted, but waived. Waiver material can be re-used free of charge without requiring a formal licence provided that the waiver conditions as set out in Figure 8.3 are observed.

Where copyright is waived this means that although copyright is asserted, the government wishes to encourage the widespread use of the material. Users are permitted to copy or publish the material in any medium without having to seek formal permission or pay a fee.

The policy with regard to Crown copyright in legislative materials (Acts and statutory instruments) can be found in OPSI guidance note 6;

- Reproductions may only be made from the official version.
- Material must be reproduced accurately and in a manner and context which is not misleading as to its intended meaning and application.
- Content must not be used in connection with advertising, endorsement or in any context which could be viewed as undignified association.
- Material must not be used in any circumstances which are knowingly or potentially libelous or slanderous of individuals, companies or organizations.
- It must be properly acknowledged – there is an appropriate set of words for this purpose which is set in the Crown copyright guidance notes available on the OPSI website.

Figure 8.3 The terms of the Crown copyright waiver

while the policy for parliamentary copyright material appears in the 'Dear Librarian' letter and OPSI guidance note 14 (which covers reproduction of bills and explanatory notes to bills). These can be found on the OPSI website (www.opsi.gov.uk).

OPSI click-use licence

OPSI has an online licence for the re-use of Crown and parliamentary copyright material. In the case of crown copyright material there are in fact two click-use licences – the core licence and the value-added licence; and there is a click-use licence to cover parliamentary copyright material.

The following guidance is provided on the OPSI website:

 Guidance on the Re-use of Crown Copyright Extracts[3]
In order to simplify the process and reduce unnecessary administration and delay for re-users of Crown copyright material, extracts of up to 250 words from official sources may be re-used without the need to apply for a licence.

. . .

This covers both core and value-added text (a list of examples of value-added text can be found on the OPSI website).[4] It does not, however, extend to:
- text that appears in tables, diagrams and forms;
- cases where a department states that the material may not be re-used. For example, material that is frequently updated and where out of date information could potentially affect the health, safety and security of individuals;
- the re-use of official imprints and departmental logos unless you have the permission of the department concerned.

. . .

You may re-use extracts of text provided that:
- it is re-used accurately;
- you identify the source and state that it is Crown copyright. If you are including the text in a publication of your own, you should use the copyright notice – Crown copyright material is reproduced with the permission of the Controller of HMSO and the Queen's Printer for Scotland;

- it is not re-used for the purpose of advertising or promoting a particular product or service;
- out of date material is not presented as though it was current.

OPSI copyright guidance

The OPSI copyright guidance notes provide further information about the material that is subject to the waiver (www.opsi.gov.uk/advice/crown-copyright/copyright-guidance/index.htm) as follows:

- Publication of Articles written by Ministers and Civil Servants
- Copyright in Public Records
- Reproduction of Court Forms
- Copyright in Works Commissioned by the Crown
- Reproduction of United Kingdom, England, Wales and Northern Ireland Primary and Secondary Legislation
- Guidance on the copying of Birth, Death, Marriage and Civil Partnership Certificates and Marriage Registers
- Reproduction of National Curriculum Material, and Literacy and Numeracy Strategy Documents, for England
- Reproduction of Government Press Notices for England, Northern Ireland and Wales
- Reproduction of National Curriculum Material for Wales/Atgynhyrchu Deunydd y Cwricwlwm Cenedlaethol ar gyfer Cymru
- Copyright and Publishing Notices
- Reproduction of Bills and Explanatory Notes to Bills of the United Kingdom Parliament
- Reproduction of the Record of Proceedings, the National Assembly for Wales/Atgynhyrchu Cofnod y Trafodion, Cynulliad Cenedlaethol Cymru
- Information Asset Register and Freedom of Information – a co-ordinated response to information access
- Freedom of Information Publication Schemes
- Reproduction of the British Passport
- Crown Copyright – an overview for government departments

- Re-use of Crown Copyright Extracts
- Waiver of Crown Copyright.

Web copyright notice

Many websites will set out in a copyright notice what users of the site are permitted to do. These terms should be respected. If you want to create a deep link to a website, you have to be careful, because it may state clearly in the terms and conditions that deep linking is not allowed. Creating a deep link in such circumstances would mean that not only were you ignoring the site's terms and conditions but also you were getting anyone who followed your deep link to do so without them even having the chance to see that they were contravening the terms of the site.

There is also a question mark over the enforceability of a set of terms and conditions which appears on a website if people have to make a point of clicking on those terms. It is best from the site owner's point of view if they design the website in a way which forces the user to look at the terms and conditions and to click on an 'I agree' button before being able to progress any further into the site.

8.1.4   Licence

Under the heading of 'licence' I am thinking specifically of licences issued by a collective licensing society acting on behalf of authors, publishers and visual artists.

In order for library and information professionals to make a legal copy for their users of material which is subject to copyright protection, if

- the copying is not covered by one of the copyright exceptions or permitted acts
- copyright clearance has not been sought from the rightsholder directly and
- the copying is not covered by a contract

there are still a number of other options available to legitimize the copying. They include:

- taking out a licence from someone who acts on behalf of the rightsholder, such as a collective licensing society
- paying a copyright fee by using the CLA sticker scheme
- paying for a copyright-cleared copy through a document supply service which is licensed by a collective licensing society.

For library and information professionals, the main collective licensing societies to consider are:

Copyright Licensing Agency Ltd
6–10 Kirby Street
London EC1N 8TS
Tel: 020 7400 3100   Website: www.cla.co.uk

Newspaper Licensing Agency
7–9 Church Road
Wellington Gate
Tunbridge Wells TN1 1NL
Tel: 01892 525273   Website: www.nla.co.uk

Design and Artists Copyright Society
Parchment House
13 Northburgh Street
London EC1V 0JP
Tel: 020 7336 8811   Website: www.dacs.co.uk
There are licensing schemes available from other organizations, such as the licence for educational establishments from the Educational Recording Agency, which covers all terrestrial broadcasting with the exception of Open University programmes:

Educational Recording Agency
New Premier House
150 Southampton Row
London WC1B 5AL
Tel: 020 7837 3222   Website: www.era.org.uk/

The indemnity offered by collective licensing schemes

Where a user enters into a licence agreement with a collective licensing organization, the licensing organization is required by law to provide an indemnity to the licensee, and this will be available provided that you observe the obligations set out in the agreement.

Section 136 of the CDPA 1988 (Implied indemnity in certain schemes and licences for reprographic copying) states:

(1) This section applies to—
  (a) schemes for licensing reprographic copying of published literary, dramatic, musical or artistic works, or the typographical arrangement of published editions, and
  (b) licences granted by licensing bodies for such copying, where the scheme or licence does not specify the works to which it applies with such particularity as to enable licensees to determine whether a work falls within the scheme or licence by inspection of the scheme or licence and the work.
(2) There is implied—
  (a) in every scheme to which this section applies an undertaking by the operator of the scheme to indemnify a person granted a licence under the scheme, and
  (b) in every licence to which this section applies an undertaking by the licensing body to indemnify the licensee, against any liability incurred by him by reason of his having infringed copyright by making or authorising the making of reprographic copies of a work in circumstances within the apparent scope of his licence.
(3) The circumstances of a case are within the apparent scope of a licence if—
  (a) it is not apparent from inspection of the licence and the work that it does not fall within the description of works to which the licence applies; and
  (b) the licence does not expressly provide that it does not extend to copyright of the description infringed.
(4) In this section "liability" includes liability to pay costs; and this section applies in relation to costs reasonably incurred by a licensee in connection with actual or contemplated proceedings

against him for infringement of copyright as it applies to sums which he is liable to pay in respect of such infringement.

(5) A scheme or licence to which this section applies may contain reasonable provision—

(a) with respect to the manner in which, and time within which, claims under the undertaking implied by this section are to be made;

(b) enabling the operator of the scheme or, as the case may be, the licensing body to take over the conduct of any proceedings affecting the amount of his liability to indemnify.

In principle, you will need authorization from the copyright owner:

- if the work is covered by copyright and/or related rights law(s)
- if the work is not in the public domain
- if your planned exploitation implies the use of all or part of the rights granted to the copyright and/or related rightsowner
- if your intended use is not covered by 'fair dealing' or by a copyright exception or permitted act specifically included in the national copyright or related rights law.

8.2 Can I copy?

It is not possible to give a straightforward 'yes' or 'no' answer to this question. The fact is that there are a large number of points to be taken into consideration (see Figure 8.4).

☑ If the written permission has been obtained from the owner of the right to copy the materials

☑ If copying falls within the regulations of a licensing agency to which your organization subscribes

☑ If you have a legal defence, for example 'fair dealing'

☒ If you don't have permission, don't have a licence from an agency or don't have a legal defence

---

Figure 8.4 Is your copying legal?

Your copying is permitted if:

- you hold the rights to copy because you are the author yourself (but note that this is not always the case as the work may have been produced as part of your paid employment and therefore your employer holds the rights, or you have signed over the rights to a publisher)
- copyright has expired
- you have permission from the rightsholder(s) or their agent; fees may or may not have to be paid to obtain this permission
- the copying falls within the terms of your organization's licences with collective licensing societies
- the copying falls within the accepted limits of 'fair dealing' for the purposes of non-commercial research, e.g. an insubstantial amount for research or private study, criticism or review, or the reporting of current events.

You should bear in mind that a person who has placed material on the internet may not have had any rights to do so in the first place, and that in copying and re-distributing the material you may well be opening yourself up to action being taken against you by the rightsholder.

8.3 Fair use and the PNAM tests

UK copyright law does not specify the exact limits of fair dealing, such as stating a specific amount of material that may be safely copied or used without permission. The reason for this is that a court would determine whether a particular act of copying could be considered to be fair dealing by looking both at the *quantity* of material copied and also at *qualitative* issues.

United States law covers not 'fair dealing', but 'fair use', and people in the USA consider four key criteria – known as PNAM – in order to determine whether it was right to rely upon the fair use provisions:

1 the *purpose* and character of the use
2 the *nature* of the copyrighted work
3 the *amount* and substantiality of the portion used in relation to the whole

4   the *market impact*, that is the effect of the use on the potential market for or value of the work.

(See summary in Table 8.1 and case study overleaf.)

Table 8.1 Checklist for fair use		
Factor	**Favouring fair use**	**Opposing fair use**
1: Purpose – the environment and character of the use	• Teaching • Multiple copies for classroom • Scholarship • Criticism • Commentary • News reporting • Parody • Transformative use • Restricted access for class use • Non-profit	• Commercial use • Entertainment use • Financial benefit • Removal of copyright notice • Unrestricted use • Reproductions
2: Nature – type of work being used	• Published work • Factual work • Non-fiction work • Directly related to use	• Unpublished work • Creative expression • Fictional work • Non-essential to use
3: Amount and substantiality of the portion used – quantitative and qualitative	• Small portion • Portion is relevant to use • Portion is not essence or heart of the entire work • Thumbnail low-resolution image	• Large portion or entire work • Portion is significant 'heart of the work' • Full-sized image
4: Effect of the use on the potential market for or value of the work	• Copy lawfully acquired • Few copies made • No significant effect on the potential market • No market for permissions	• Permissions available • Licensing available • Unrestricted public access • Unlimited term of use

These four factors have a statutory basis, as set out in section 107 of the (US) Copyright Act of 1976. The section states in full:

Notwithstanding the provisions of sections 106 and 106A, the fair use of a copyrighted work, including such use by reproduction in copies or phonorecords or by any other means specified by that section, for purposes such as criticism, comment, news reporting, teaching (including multiple copies for classroom use), scholarship, or research, is not an infringement of copyright. In determining whether the use made of a work in any particular case is a fair use, the factors to be considered shall include—

(1) the purpose and character of the use, including whether such use is of a commercial nature or is for nonprofit educational purposes;
(2) the nature of the copyrighted work;
(3) the amount and substantiality of the portion used in relation to the copyrighted work as a whole; and
(4) the effect of the use upon the potential market for or value of the copyrighted work. [In recent years this has been considered to be the most heavily weighted of the four factors.]

The fact that a work is unpublished shall not itself bar a finding of fair use if such finding is made upon consideration of all the above factors.

If the use is for the purposes stated in the statute, and if the term of copyright protection is still in effect, each of the four factors must be applied in order to use the work without seeking permission. The fair use test is applicable to single and multiple copies for the classroom. While any single factor may not lend itself to a fair use, the combined analysis of the other factors can tip the balance for an overall fair use.

CASE STUDY Applying the four-factor test

In order to illustrate the use of the PNAM test, the following is a consideration of how this would apply in the case of Lowry's Reports v Legg Mason [2003].

Background: Legg Mason shared one paid $700 subscription to Lowry's Market Trend Analysis with more than 1300 employees over the company's intranet.

In mid-2003 the federal district court in Maryland found Legg Mason liable to Lowry's for breach of contract and wilful copyright infringement.

Outcome: Legg Mason was required to pay newsletter publisher Lowry's Reports $19,725,270 in damages and lost subscription fees. Legg Mason went back to court in February 2004 seeking a reduction in the award for damages, but instead the figure was upheld.

In the Lowry's Reports v Legg Mason case the court applied these four factors in order to evaluate Legg Mason's fair use claim:

- *Purpose*: The commercial nature of the defendant's business leans against a finding of fair use.
- *Nature:* The nature of the newsletter is that of a factual work which contains useful information gathered by the publisher. Each issue is often only four pages long, and an annual subscription to the title cost $700.
- *Amount or substantiality:* The amount and substantiality factor goes against Legg Mason because the company was reproducing each issue in its entirety.
- *Market impact:* The effect on the market also weighs against Legg Mason because Lowry's is a small publisher which restricts subscriptions to individual subscribers. Thus, the court found there was no fair use. ■

8.4 Copyright declaration forms

Where a librarian of a prescribed[5] (not-for-profit) library undertakes copying on behalf of library users, there is a legal requirement to ask the requester to complete a copyright declaration form before the copy is made.

The wording of the declaration forms requires the user to sign to say that the copying is for a non-commercial purpose or private study.

There are two types of form, one to cover the use of published works and the other to cover the use of unpublished works. There are model declaration forms available to use from the Libraries and Archives Copyright Alliance website:

- Form A must be used when providing privileged copies to users published works
  (www.cilip.org.uk/policyadvocacy/copyright/formsandposters/forms/forma.htm).
- Form B must be used when providing privileged copies to users from unpublished works
  (www.cilip.org.uk/policyadvocacy/copyright/formsandposters/forms/formb.htm).

The declaration form provides the librarian with an indemnity. If the regulations have been followed correctly, the librarian is protected from accusations of infringement. It is therefore imperative that you keep the forms. Taking into account the Limitation Act (1980), the forms should be kept for up to six years plus the current year.

Librarians must remember that they are not expected to police what individuals sign on the declaration forms. They should be careful not to decide for people that the copying is for a non-commercial purpose, even if they are asked to give users advice in interpreting the form. The decision rests with the user. The best thing to do would be to direct library users to the document 'Changes to UK Copyright Law: a joint note from the British Library and The Copyright Licensing Agency', or to the CILIP copyright posters. If you were to advise a user that a particular use was non-commercial, and a court subsequently decided that your advice was incorrect, you could be held jointly liable with the user for that instance of copyright infringement.

There are no declaration forms for the other copyright exceptions, only for 'library privilege'. The UK Intellectual Property Office feels that it is preferable to keep the number of forms to a minimum. You can always devise your own form to cover other exceptions if you so wish, but these would carry no statutory indemnity.

8.5 Creative Commons

Open content licensing is an alternative to the existing model of copyright. One example of this is Creative Commons, which defines the range of possibilities between full copyright on the one hand and the public domain on the other. Creative Commons can be summarized as offering access to content with 'some rights reserved' as opposed to all rights being reserved.

In order to make it quick and easy to identify what can be done with content licensed by Creative Commons, it makes use of symbols. These identify the following permissions or restrictions as listed on the Creative Commons website (http://creativecommons.org/about/licences):

- **Attribution**. You let others copy, distribute, display, and perform your copyrighted work — and derivative works based upon it — but only if they give credit the way you request.
- **Noncommercial**. You let others copy, distribute, display, and

perform your work — and derivative works based upon it — but for noncommercial purposes only

- **No Derivative Works**. You let others copy, distribute, display, and perform only verbatim copies of your work, not derivative works based upon it.
- **Share Alike**. You allow others to distribute derivative works only under a license identical to the license that governs your work.

Note

A license cannot feature both the Share Alike and No Derivative Works options. The Share Alike requirement applies only to derivative works.

One way of overcoming copyright headaches with content would be to seek out material which is made available under an open content licence such as a Creative Commons licence. But you would need to be careful to check that the licence covered the particular copying activity that you had in mind, as there is a range of different licences available.

There are a number of search tools to help users seek out content which is governed by a Creative Commons licence. These include:

http://search.creativecommons.org/
http://search.yahoo.com/cc

In addition, even though for most people Google is the search engine of choice, most users of the Google search engine will not have noticed that on the advanced search screen (www.google.co.uk/advanced_search?hl=en) there is an option 'Usage rights', with a drop-down list containing the following options:

- not filtered by license
- free to use or share
- free to use or share, even commercially
- free to use, share or modify
- free to use, share or modify, even commercially.

This feature is intended to help users to find published content – including music, photos, movies, books and educational materials – that they can share or modify above and beyond fair use. If you set the search filter to 'free to use or share', it is possible to retrieve a set of search results for material that you can copy or redistribute. It is important to point out, though, that Google does leave it up to the users to verify the terms under which the content is made available and to make their own assessments as to whether these terms are lawfully applied to the content.

8.6 Public domain

According to Wikipedia,[6] the public domain 'comprises the body of knowledge and innovation (especially creative works such as writing, art, music, and inventions) in relation to which no person or other legal entity can establish or maintain proprietary interests within a particular legal jurisdiction'.

In order to overcome the problems associated with obtaining the necessary permission to copy material which is protected by copyright, it is worth considering the use of public domain content. However, even that is not quite as straightforward as it may at first sound. If a publisher had recently published a new copy of a work that was in the public domain, you wouldn't be able just to go ahead and scan or photocopy the whole work. That is because, while the text is no longer protected by copyright, the typographical arrangement will nevertheless be protected for 25 years; and the work may well be accompanied by a new preface, introduction and other preliminary content which will also be protected by copyright.

The Europe-wide project funded by the European Commission known as Communia, the European Thematic Network on the Public Domain in the Digital Age (www.ec.europa.eu/information_society/activities/ econtentplus/projects/psi/communia/index_en.htm), was launched in 2007. The rationale behind this digital network is that it provides an opportunity to share and build on the global pool of knowledge in the public domain.

The Public Domain Works database (www.publicdomainworks.net) is an open registry of works that are in the public domain. It is focused on sound recordings because a copyright term extension for sound recordings in Europe is currently under debate. It is anticipated that the database will in due course be expanded to cover all types of cultural works which are covered by copyright.

Public Domain Works advises users on the copyright status of a particular sound track they wish to re-use, and this encourages creators and entrepreneurs to build on our cultural history. The tool is only at the alpha stage so far, which means that it needs a lot of work before its full launch.

8.7 Keeping within the terms of licence agreements

Even if you have a licence with a collective licensing society, you will still need to be mindful of the limitations of the licence agreement.

Check the terms of the licensing scheme in order to make sure that you are familiar with them and that you fully understand them.

In the case of the Copyright Licensing Agency, for example, you need to make sure:

- the item you want to copy is not on the excluded works list (or in the case of US publications, that it is from one of the participating publishers)
- that it is published in one of the licensed territories (UK, Argentina, Australia, Austria, Belgium, Canada [inc. Quebec], Denmark, Finland, France, Germany, Greece, Hong Kong, Iceland, Ireland, Jamaica, Luxembourg, Mexico, the Netherlands, New Zealand, Norway, Singapore, South Africa, Spain, Sweden, Switzerland [including Liechtenstein] and participating US publishers are currently covered)[7]
- that you stay within the approved limits – these will differ from one CLA licence to another (for example, the limits in the business licence are:
  no more than 5% of any item of Licensed Material, or:
  (a) in the case of a periodical publication, one whole article; or
  (b) in the case of a published report of judicial proceedings, the entire report of a single case; or
  (c) in the case of a book, one chapter).

Another point worth checking is whether the licence agreement makes a distinction between hard copy and electronic items in the repertoire of material covered. For example, in the case of the Newspaper Licensing

Agency, the digital licence doesn't cover News International content, whereas its content is covered in the basic (hard copy) licence.[8] In the case of the CLA, many licences permit the scanning of content, but the making of digital (i.e. scanned) copies of material is restricted to UK content.

Notes

1   When a single copy of an item is made under the exception of fair dealing for non-commercial research or private study, the safe copying limits are usually taken to be: one chapter or 5% (whichever is the greater) or one journal article. However, the fair dealing exception as set out in the CDPA 1988 is not as specific as this – it certainly doesn't, for example, give a set percentage that is acceptable in all circumstances

2   www.cilip.org/uk/policyadvocacy/copyright/formsandposters/posters_pics.htm.

3   The guidance can be found on the OPSI website at www.opsi.gov.uk/advice/crown-copyright/copyright-guidance/re-use-of-crown-copyright-extracts.htm.

4   www.opsi.gov.uk/click-use/value-added-licence-information/examples-of-value-added-material.htm.

5   The list of prescribed libraries is set out in Schedule 1 of the Library Regulations (SI 1989/1212). It includes public libraries; national libraries; libraries in educational establishments; parliamentary and government libraries; local authority libraries; and libraries whose main purpose is to encourage the study of a wide range of subjects (including libraries outside the UK).

6   http://en.wikipedia.org/wiki/Public_domain.

7   For an up-to-date listing of the countries covered by the CLA licence, see www.cla.co.uk/licenceinformation_listofexcludedcategoriesandexcludedworks.php.

8   The NLA's eClips service, which covers digital versions of press clippings, and which is offered to press clippings agencies, does, however, include News International's content.

9
The copyright clearance process

In order to be able to copy material, you first need to ensure that you have the necessary rights or permissions in order to do so. Such authorization could, for example, be in the form of one of the copyright exceptions or permitted acts; it could be through a licence which you already have with a collecting society; or it could be some other form of authorization such as the Crown copyright waiver. If you do not currently have the required authorization to copy, then you will need to arrange for the rights to be cleared. It can take time to locate rightsowners, especially if the original publisher turns out to have sold the rights to someone else. This chapter deals with the whole process of obtaining copyright clearance, including a number of practical suggestions for tracking down rightsowners.

The first question to ask would be: Is clearance required? Permission may not be necessary, and this could be the case for a number of reasons:

- The material is in the public domain (see Chapter 8, section 8.6) (but this would only apply where both the typographical rights and the copyright relating to the content had expired).
- Government publications are covered by the Crown copyright waiver.
- The copying may be covered by an existing licence held by your organization.
- Copyright is not required because of the publisher's policy – for

example, some journal publishers are willing to grant free permissions to digitize where the requesting institution holds a subscription.

The rightsholder is the ultimate source for all permissions. It is worth bearing in mind that there is no formal process which a creator has to go through before copyright is granted. Instead, copyright is an automatic right. The consequence is that there is no comprehensive register which can be used to locate the creator or rightsholder in a work in order to seek their explicit permission to copy material.

The question arises, then, as to how to find out who holds the rights. The copyright owner may be:

- the creator of the material or his/her heirs
- the creator's employer
- anyone else to whom the rights in the material have been sold, or otherwise transferred or licensed.

If the creator or owner of the rights in a work died less than 70 years ago, the rights in that work will have been transferred to someone else. This could either be through a will or through inheritance. In the case of a will (or testamentary deposition), the document will indicate to whom the rights in the material have been given. However, if there was no will, or if the creator of the work has not specified where the rights in the material should go, the normal rules of inheritance will apply. Table 9.1 lists collecting societies and other organizations representing rightsowners.

9.1 Pre-clearance issues and preparation

It will be necessary to:

- determine the copyright status for each of the items to be copied
- determine the scope of content and the full range of permissions and rights you need for your purposes, especially if there are multiple copyrights in a work
- be clear as to how much you are prepared to pay for the copying, and stick within the limits you decide on.

Table 9.1 Collecting societies and other organizations representing rightsowners

Organization	Telephone	Website
Copyright Licensing Agency	020 7400 3100	www.cla.co.uk
Newspaper Licensing Agency	01892 525273	www.nla.co.uk
Educational Recording Agency	020 7837 3222	www.era.org.uk
Design Artists Copyright Society	020 7336 8811	www.dacs.co.uk
Mechanical Copyright Protection Society and the Performing Right Society	020 7580 5544	www.mcps-prs-alliance.co.uk
Open University	0845 300 6090	www.open.ac.uk
Copyright Clearance Center (USA)	001 978 750 8400	www.copyright.com
Authors' Licensing and Collecting Society	020 7264 5700	www.alcs.co.uk

9.2 Clearing the required rights

Getting permission to copy isn't always a straightforward matter. Consider, for example, the following scenarios. What would you do if:

- the rights-holder does not reply?
- you cannot trace one out of the three rightsholders?
- the rightsholder replies and asks for a fee which is too high?
- the rightsholder replies giving permission – but not for the third-party material within the main work?
- the rightsholder replies but the permission to digitize is time restricted?
- the rightsholder gives permission, but not for simultaneous access?
- the rightsholder requires you to supply them with a copy of your digitization?

If getting the necessary rights clearances turns out to be problematic, you have to decide whether or not you are still going to go ahead and copy. There are two key questions at this point which you must ask yourself:

1 What is the likelihood of legal action?
2 Are you willing to take the risk?

If you have tried all avenues to trace the publisher and the author, and failed, then the decision to copy the materials comes down to a risk assessment.

Imagine, by way of illustration, that an educational establishment has decided to undertake a digitization project. Considerable time and effort has been spent in getting the necessary rights clearances, but inevitably this has not been possible in all cases. The educational establishment has reached the point where it now has to decide whether or not to go ahead and digitize those items for which it has not been able to track down the rightsholder.

There is undoubtedly a risk involved in going ahead without the necessary permissions in place. The question is, how significant are the risks involved? If anyone is willing to take risks, they should at least do everything they can to minimize those risks, and in this particular instance that would mean taking account of the following considerations:

- Are the materials being digitized with an educational purpose in mind?
- Has the decision to digitize only been made after determined efforts to locate rightsholders have been undertaken?
- Have the efforts which were made to track down the rightsowners been carefully documented?
- Were advertisements placed in local newspapers or relevant trade journals in order to try and alert possible rightsholders to the project plans?

Take another example. You are the author of a book, and want to include several items for which the rightsowner cannot be traced. You have undertaken a time-consuming search for the owners of the copyright, without success, and have kept a detailed log of the steps you took as part of that search. You have therefore decided to go ahead and include the material in question, and have included a statement to the effect that

> Every effort has been made to trace the copyright owner of this material, and anyone claiming copyright should get in touch with xxx.

It is extremely important that you keep copies of any documentation relating to the clearance (or not) of any material used, so that you are able to prove that you did your best to trace the rightsholder, and that you have been trying to act in good faith, in case of claims.

For a major digitization project involving thousands of individual items, making thorough attempts to trace rightsowners, and keeping a detailed record of the steps you took, may not be practical. That is why the issue of orphan works – or works for which the rightsowner cannot be located – has risen up the agenda recently (see section 9.3.2 in this chapter).

In its response to the *Gowers Review*, the National Council on Archives cited an example of a historian who tried to obtain the necessary permissions before having a book published:

> A local historian published a book with photographs all of which he had permission to use except for one, for which he was unable to find the copyright owner, although he spent considerable effort in his search. Deciding to go ahead without permission he had the book printed with the usual calls for the owner. Immediately the copyright owner demanded £20,000 for using his photograph without permission. The local historian had to pay a much smaller payment but had to pay.[1]

This story illustrates a number of problems that arise when someone contacts a rightsowner for permission. There is absolutely no obligation on the part of the rightsowner to respond to a request from someone to use their content. And if the requester doesn't hear back, they have to bear in mind that by sending in a written request seeking the necessary permission, they have alerted the rightsowner of their wish to copy the content.

If you do decide that it is worth taking the risk, you may wish to set aside an appropriate fee for the use of the work, which you then put into a special bank account, because you have to bear in mind that if the rightsholder does appear they will be likely to expect some form of payment. Indeed, they may even consider suing you for infringement of their rights.

9.3 Tracing copyright holders

One useful source of information on tracking down copyright holders is the Book Trust's factsheet on locating copyright holders.

Figure 9.1 outlines a number of useful routes for tracing rightsowners, whether they be authors, publishers or companies. Another possibility, which people may well overlook, is to use a company which specializes in locating people.

9.3.1   Tracing the rightsowner for American content

The Thomson Corporation's Dialog online service has a file on US copyrights. It is file 120 on the Dialog service. A factsheet about the database

---

Publishers

For a work that has been commercially published, the starting point for permission seeking will be the publisher. If, for whatever reason, they are not the rightsholder, then the next step will be to try to locate the author.

Check with the current or most recent publisher. If they don't hold the rights, they can generally refer you to whoever they think holds the rights.

Various directories of publishers

Ulrich's Periodicals Directory, www.ulrichsweb.com/ulrichsweb
Booksellers Association publisher directory,
    www.booksellers.org.uk/publisher_dir/directory.asp
Association of American University Presses, http://aaupnet.org
Bowker's *Books in Print*, www.booksinprint.com
Publishers Association, www.publishers.org.uk
Publishers Licensing Society, www.pls.org.uk
Welsh Book Council, www.cllc.org.uk

Authors
*   Biographers of the author.
*   WATCH (Writers Artists and their Copyright Holders) database (http://tyler.hrc.utexas.edu/). This contains primarily the names and addresses of copyright holders or contact persons for authors and artists whose archives are housed, in whole or in part, in libraries and archives in North America and the UK. The objective in making the database available is to provide information to scholars about whom to contact for permission to publish text and images that still enjoy copyright protection.
*   Author societies such as the Society of Authors (www.societyofauthors.org) or ALCS (www.alcs.co.uk).
*   In the USA, the Authors Registry (http://authorsregistry.org).

Figure 9.1 Tracing copyright holders *(continued on next page)*

Consider also using a people search company.

Databases of authors

www.societyofauthors.org and go to FIND AN AUTHOR. This is the Society's database of members and their specialisms.

www.artscape.org.uk – has details writers and artists, and the site also includes the NAWE (National Association of Writers in Education) database

www.contactanauthor.co.uk

www.nibweb.co.uk – the Network for Information Book Writers and Editors

www.readingagency.org.uk – writers in libraries

www.ncll.org.uk – the National Centre for Language and Literacy

www.applesandsnakes.org – poets

www.childrensdiscovery.org.uk – writers in schools

www.expertsources.co.uk

www.literaturetraining.com

www.ecademy.com

Defunct companies

When a company goes out of business or ceases trading, any copyright it may own continues for the normal period of copyright duration. The rights are part of the assets of the company, and may be sold or otherwise dealt with by the company or its liquidator. The Gowers Review refers to 'abandonware', where businesses go bankrupt or merge and copyright ownership information can be lost.

For defunct commercial bodies, check the Companies House website (www.companieshouse.gov.uk) and select WebCHeck. It is possible to search a number of different indexes:

• current/recently dissolved names
• dissolved names
• previous names
• proposed names.

FOB file – Firms Out of Business (http://fob-file.com) supplements the WATCH database.

Figure 9.1 Tracing copyright holders (*continued from previous page*)

and what it covers can be found at http://library.dialog.com/bluesheets/html/bl0120.html.

According to Dialog's Bluesheet,

> U.S. Copyrights, produced by The Dialog Corporation, provides access to registration details for all active copyright and mask-work registrations on file at the U.S. Copyright Office. The database has been designed primarily as a fast screening tool for checking the ownership and registration status of a particular work. The database is also useful for checking a particular individual's or entity's portfolio of registered works.

The US Copyright Office offers a fee-based search service for people who are interested in investigating whether a work is under copyright protection and, if so, the facts of the copyright. For a fee of $150 per hour or fraction thereof, the Office will search its public records and provide a report of its findings. The Office can provide an estimate of the total search fee before conducting the search, based on the information it is given by the enquirer.

The Copyright Office does say 'Please be advised that there are limitations on searches and that searches are not always conclusive' (www.copyright.gov/forms/ search_estimate.html).

The US Copyright Office also produces a circular (circular number 22) called *How to Investigate the Copyright Status of a Work* (www.copyright.gov/circs/circ22.html).

9.3.2   Orphan works

Orphan works are works which are protected by copyright but for which the present owner of the copyright is unknown and unknowable by reasonable enquiry. They pose a major problem for digitization projects which are intended to result in the availability of large quantities of copyright material online.

The UK government does not currently have the power to introduce an exception into copyright legislation to cover orphan works, because this would first require a change at EU level. The fact is that, as things stand, European legislation does not currently allow for a simple exception which would permit the unlicensed use of orphan works, whether after attempting to trace the rightsowner or not.

The *Gowers Review* was certainly mindful of the problem of 'orphan works', and put forward three recommendations relating to the topic, as shown in Table 9.2.

Table 9.3 shows the two main solutions which have been put forward to resolve the problem of orphan works. They are not mutually exclusive and could co-exist.

It may, however, be necessary to consider a third option in order to cater for mass digitization projects, because neither of the above solutions adequately addresses the full range of issues that can arise.

Table 9.2 *Gowers Review* recommendations on orphan works

Recommendation	Timetable for initial action
Recommendation 13: Propose a provision for orphan works to the European Commission, amending Directive 2001/29/EC.	Recommendation is to the European Commission
Recommendation 14a: The Patent Office should issue clear guidance on the parameters of a 'reasonable search' for orphan works, in consultation with rightsholders, collecting societies, rightsowners and archives, when an orphan works exception comes into being.	Will be dependent on outcome of Recommendation 13
Recommendation 14b: The Patent Office should establish a voluntary register of copyright; either on its own, or through partnerships with database holders, by 2008.	End 2008

Table 9.3 Solutions to the problem of orphan works

	Advantages	Disadvantages
The licensing route	One stop shop. If the copyright owner does subsequently appear, there would be a mechanism in place for them to be recompensed.	There are certain types of material such as business letters and many other manuscript materials in archives, libraries and museums where there was never any intention on the part of the creator to create a work which was to be exploited commercially. The authors and their descendants will never be members of licensing societies and therefore those societies are unable to license the use of such works.
The copyright exception route (so long as a 'reasonable enquiry' has been undertaken in order to identify and locate the copyright owner)	Avoids the need to take out a licence agreement for occasional, ad hoc copying.	For a major digitization project it would be totally impractical to undertake a diligent search for huge numbers of items.

If one were to rely on a copyright exception requiring a 'reasonable enquiry' to be made in order to identify and locate the rightsowner, this would be completely impractical for a mass digitization project where clearance for many tens of thousands of items might be required. Nor would the licensing route provide a solution, because in a number of instances – for example in the case of unpublished literary material such as private letters and diaries – it wouldn't be possible for a licensing organization to include these in its repertoire. One has to remember that the licensing bodies are at present only able to issue licences where they have been given a mandate to do so by their members. By their very nature, in the case of orphan works, there are no known rightsowners able to give the necessary mandates. As a result, either the licensing bodies would have to be willing to issue licences without such a mandate or legislation would be needed authorizing them to do so.

In 2007 the British Library produced a set of seven principles[2] on which any solution to the problem of orphan works in an era of mass digitization should be based:

1 Clear attribution of authorship
2 Mixed economy (by which is meant a role for the collecting societies while at the same time having a copyright exception
3 Search guidelines (which would cater for a wide range of types of material)
4 Scalable guidelines for a 'reasonable search'
5 Safe harbour status for public bodies
6 Consensus on historical cut-off points
7 Preventative action (to ensure that the creation of future orphan works is prevented).

All parties need to have legal certainty with regard to the use of orphan works. On the one hand, users need to be able to feel safe to use material which falls into the category of orphan works. On the other hand, licensors (where appropriate) should feel able to issue licences for use across Europe.

What constitutes a 'reasonable search'?

If a copyright exception were to be introduced based on the user under-taking a 'reasonable search', it would be absolutely essential for the Intellectual Property Office to provide a set of guidelines on the 'due diligence' that would be required. The guidelines would need to be elaborated, based on what might be considered to be reasonable under the circumstances, and the question arises as to whether they would need to be tailored to meet the needs of the various sectors while at the same time being compatible with one another. There would certainly be a problem if the guidelines were too prescriptive.

Every 'reasonable' effort should be made in order to trace the right-sholder; and it is essential to keep good records of your efforts. If you are challenged about the copying that you have done, this will help to show that you were acting in good faith and had made reasonable efforts to try and track down the rightsholder.

The following prerequisites would need to be fulfilled when considering the possibility of using orphan works:

1   A user wishes to make good faith use of a work with an unclear copyright status.
2   Due diligence has been observed in trying to find out who the rightsholders are and/or locate them.
3   The user wishes to use the work in a clearly defined manner.
4   It is up to the user to clear the rights with an appropriate body.

In the USA, a proposed bill[3] (which didn't pass into law) was issued in 2006, and that bill included a set of standards for a *reasonably diligent search*. It said that such a search includes the use of reasonably available expert assistance and reasonably available technology, which may include, if reasonable under the circumstances, resources for which a charge or subscription fee is imposed.

> . . . the Register of Copyrights shall receive, maintain and make available to the public, including through the internet, information from authoritative sources, such as industry guidelines, statements of best practices, and other relevant documents, that is designed to assist users in conducting and documenting a reasonably diligent search under this

sub-section. Such information may include:

i.   the records of the Copyright Office that are relevant to identifying and locating copyright owners

ii. other sources of copyright ownership information reasonably available to users

iii. methods to identify copyright ownership information associated with a work

iv. sources of reasonably available technology tools and reasonably available expert assistance; and

v.   best practices for documenting a reasonably diligent search

For content in electronic form some people suggest that metadata can and should be used in order to identify the relevant rightsowner(s). However, given that copyright in a work is a property which can be bought and sold, it would mean that for people to be able to rely on its accuracy, the metadata would need to be up to date, and to reflect any ownership changes.

Further information

Report on orphan works: a report of the Register of Copyrights (January 2006) United States Copyright Office, www.copyright.gov/orphan/orphan-report.pdf.
The Orphan Works Act of 2006, http://thomas.loc.gov/cgi-bin/query/z?c109:H.R.5439.
US Copyright Office web page on orphan works, www.copyright.gov/orphan/.

9.3.3   Copyright Clearance Center

The Copyright Clearance Center is the main collective licensing society for the USA and it offers a number of copyright clearance services to its customers. These include:

•   The 'Digital Permission Service', which grants permission to fax documents or to place them on the internet, an intranet or extranet. It covers most American publishers and some UK ones too.

- Rightsphere,[4] a rights advisory and management tool which manages all rights issues in a single location and addresses the question 'What can I do with this content?'
- Rightslink, which enables customers to order reprints and request permissions directly from a rightsowners' website, providing instant service; and allows rightsowners to automate their licensing processes and generate new revenue.

9.3.4   HERON

Higher and further education institutions need to be able to provide access to electronic texts and to develop virtual learning environments (VLEs), so that they are better able to cater for the needs of part-time students and distance learners.

The HERON service (www.heron.ingenta.com), which is run on a commercial basis, is able to organize copyright clearance for subscribing higher education institutions, and has an average clearance rate of around 90% of all requests for text-based materials. It is a one-stop-shop for copyright clearance and digitization, enabling universities and colleges to provide access to key learning materials for all their students, wherever they are based. Heron primarily deals with book and journal extracts. It has developed a resource bank of over 2.5 million digitized extracts for rapid re-use (subject to copyright permissions).

9.4   Sample forms

If you will be requesting copyright clearance from rightsholders regularly you should consider developing a standard form for this purpose (see Figures 9.2 and 9.3). This does need careful consideration, though. The length of the document is a vital factor. Anything which is too long, or contains too much legalese, or which tries to assert too many rights, may put off potential rightsholders.

Name: _____

Address: _____

_____

_____

_____

I consent and agree that (name of institution), its employees or agents have the right to interview, photograph or video me (and/or my property) for possible inclusion in ____ (details of the website/package).

I release to (name of institution), its employees or agents, the right to use, at their discretion, the material in print or digital form within the above context for the educational purposes of staff and students at (name of institution).

I agree that the materials may be used for other non-commercial purposes at the discretion of _____ (name of institution).

I am at least 18 years of age, have read and understand the above statements and am authorized to execute this agreement.

Signed _____

Date _____

If we consider at a later stage the commercial exploitation of the materials, we would not go ahead without first seeking your permission. Unless otherwise stated your name and contact details will be kept confidential.

Figure 9.2 Sample copyright release form

You may need a selection of documents, for example:

- checklists
- permissions letters
- contracts
- chaser letters.

XYZ company provides its staff and clients with links to useful websites through its extranet. It is our practice to link to the home page of other websites using a text link, providing full acknowledgement and opening the link up in a separate browser window.

Often, however, it would be more useful if our staff and clients were able to link directly to a page within a website. We are therefore writing to you in order to request permission to make a deep link to the URL listed below:

www.abc.com/directory/subdirectory/document.html

In order to avoid the need to contact you for each individual link, please could you indicate below whether you are willing to give us blanket permission to make further deep links to pages on your website if we wish to add further links from our site.

a. Yes, but only if the links are added to an intranet or other networked resource which is not accessible externally.
b. Yes, regardless of whether the links are placed on an internally or externally accessible site.

Many thanks for your assistance.

Figure 9.3 Obtaining permission to deep link

Listed below are a few sources for sample documentation which may be useful:

- www.copyright.iupui.edu/_permitintro.htm from Indiana University, which provides links to a selection of permission letters for different types of activity
- An example of a standard form for permission seeking on page 73 of Sandy Norman's book *Practical Copyright for Information Professionals* (Norman, 2004)
- *The Copyright Permission and Libel Handbook* by Lloyd Jassin and Steven Schechter has many examples of permissions letters and other documentation (Jassin and Schechter, 1998)
- Copyright permission form letter (University of Tennessee),

www.utc.edu/Administration/WalkerTeachingResourceCenter/
FacultyDevelopment/Copyright/
- How to secure permission to use copyrighted works (Indiana
  University), www.copyright.iupui.edu/permsec.htm
- Getting practical with IPR in e-learning (includes rights tracker
  forms),
  http://trustdr.ulster.ac.uk/outputs/gettingPracticalWithIPR.php
- Permission request form for classroom/course use, www.nacs.org/
  common/copyright/permissionrequest.pdf
- Copyright permission request form,
  https://util.aicpa.org/feedback/cpyright.htm
- FPA copyright permission form, www.fpa.org.uk/attachments/
  published/305/fpa%20copyright%20permission%20form.doc
- Obtaining permission to use copyright material,
  www.copyrightservice.co.uk/copyright/p13_permission
- Copyright or intellectual property policies,
  http://connect.educause.edu/term_view/
  Copyright%2Bor%2BIntellectual%2BProperty%2BPolicies.

Given the differences between UK and US law, I should point out that a
number of the above sources are American.

There are many examples on the web of legal agreements authorizing
the licensee to deep link to the licensor's website. See, for example:

- Connecting to other websites (includes a deep linking agreement),
  http://fairuse.stanford.edu/Copyright_and_Fair_Use_Overview/cha
  pter6/6-c.html
- Project Management Institute – linking agreement,
  www.pmi.org/Pages/LinkingAgreement.aspx.

Further information

Dunning, Alastair (2004) Tracing Copyright Holders: how two
  digitisation projects coped with copyright for historical material,
  http://ahds.ac.uk/creating/case-studies/tracing-copyright/.
Jassin, L. and Schechter, S. (1998) The Copyright Permission and
  Libel Handbook, Wiley.

Norman, Sandy (2004) *Practical Copyright for Information Professionals: the CILIP handbook*, Facet Publishing.

Pedley, Paul (2007) Copyright and Images, *CILIP Update*, May.

Notes

1 www.hm-treasury.gov.uk/media/9/A/national_council_on_archives_ 436_93. pdf.

2 The seven principles are set out in greater detail in *EBLIDA News*, **17**, October 2007, www.eblida.org/index.php?page=eblida-update.

3 HR 5439, 109th Congress, 2d Sess. (2006), The Orphan Works Act of 2006.

4 www.copyright.com/ccc/viewPage.do?pageCode=bu11.

10

Practical steps you can take to stay within copyright law

The best approach to staying within copyright law is to be pro-active, building copyright compliance into everyday processes. If you don't operate on that basis, but rely instead on a reactive approach whereby you respond to problems as and when they arise, then you will certainly be at far greater risk of being accused of copyright infringement. In short, I don't think it would be a good idea to work on the basis that you ask for forgiveness afterwards.

When you take a pro-active approach, you will be better able to show that you have done what you can to obey the law if, for example, you are able to demonstrate:

- that you have clear policies in place to ensure compliance with copyright law
- that you have a range of licences covering your copying activities
- that you maintain records of any attempts to obtain the necessary clearance of rights.

10.1 Copyright posters and notices

One obvious step to take is to ensure that you place posters prominently next to photocopiers, scanners, computer terminals, or for that matter any other equipment on which copyright protected material is likely to be copied.

CILIP produces two kinds of posters (see www.cilip.org.uk/policyadvocacy/copyright/formsandposters/posters.htm). Its gold poster has been designed for display beside photocopying and optical scanning machines; and its blue poster, which covers downloading from databases or from the internet, which is designed for display alongside computer workstations and printers.

Licensees of the Copyright Licensing Agency can place next to photocopiers:

- the CLA's copyright notices
- the CLA's excluded works list (www.cla.co.uk/licenceinformation_listofexcludedcategoriesandexcludedworks.php) and
- the 'List of US participating publishers in the CLA/CCC agreement' (www.cla.co.uk/us_participating_publishers.php).

10.2 Staff training and awareness

In order to raise awareness of the issues involved in copyright compliance, you may find it useful to organize some staff training. If you hold the training in-house, this gives you the opportunity to tailor it to your organizational policy and to cover the sorts of questions that regularly come up. The training course can also remind people of the key person within the organization who deals with copyright queries. The topics which people regularly ask about can be developed into a set of frequently asked questions which can be posted on the organization's intranet (see Figure 10.1 for example).

External training is available either through copyright consultants or through training companies. If you do employ an external consultant, you will need to consider whether they have the right sort of expertise to suit your organization. Do they, for example, have experience in and knowledge of the sector that you work in; and do they have a detailed knowledge of copyright law as it relates to the types of content that you use most frequently? For example, the needs of a commercial organization such as a law firm or an accountancy firm would be very different from those of a publicly funded archive collection or of a specialist collection of audiovisual materials in an educational establishment. When planning the training course programme, you will also need to negotiate with the

One question which people have asked me a number of times relates to liability for copyright infringement: if an employee carried out an act of copyright infringement, would it be the employee or the employer who was liable?

It is true that employers are vicariously liable for the acts of their employees and that consequently they are liable for copyright infringements which are committed by their employees in the course of employment. The employer could have an injunction served on them to prevent infringement of copyright taking place on their premises, they could be required to pay damages, and they could also be held criminally liable.

An employee is under a contractual duty of fidelity and that means, among other things, not committing illegal acts in the course of employment.

If the staff handbook says something along the lines 'Don't reproduce copyrighted material without authorization from the copyright owner' and 'The use of any pirated material is a breach of company policy', then you need to bear in mind that an act of copyright infringement could constitute a breach of the company's rules. The handbook may well spell out the consequences: 'Please note that any staff member found to be in breach of the terms of this code of conduct may be subject to disciplinary action and, depending on the severity of the offence, may be dismissed.'

An employer will not be liable for an act committed by one of its employees if the employer can prove that it took such steps as were reasonably practicable to prevent the employee from doing that act, or from doing in the course of his or her employment acts of that description.

Personal liability of directors is limited to their actual knowledge. This has been criticized by rightsowners and their representatives, who say that it allows directors to avoid any possibility of personal liability by issuing, but not enforcing, 'no copying' policies and subsequently denying knowledge of any infringements that are committed by their staff.

Were the librarian to advise a user that a particular act of copying was acceptable, and it subsequently turned out to be an infringing copy, the librarian would be jointly liable for the infringement. Information professionals need to be aware that infringing acts can take place on their premises and that they can be held liable for them.

Figure 10.1 Who has liability for infringements – the employer or employee?

consultant on what areas are to be covered. Don't, for example, ask for a basic overview of copyright issues if you want the trainer to cover very specialist areas.

10.3 Organizational documentation

Your organization may have a copyright policy which is set out in documents such as:

- statement on responsible use of the intranet
- a guide to copyright written by the in-house lawyer
- a set of frequently asked questions which deals with the typical uses your organization makes of copyright-protected material.

If not, you should think about developing such a policy and making it widely available within your organization. Loughborough University's website has a set of links that contains many examples of copyright policy statements and publicity material generated by universities. These pages originate from Elizabeth Gadd's research entitled 'Clearing the Way' (www.lboro.ac.uk/library/crightpages.html).

It would be worth considering whether to undertake an audit of your organization's copying activities (see Chapter 4, section 4.1).

Building copyright compliance into your organization's routine practices will be far easier than dealing with it on an ad hoc basis at a later stage. For example, do you ever purchase e-books, electronic journals, reports or articles in digital form on behalf of your users? And do you forward them by e-mail to your users? If so, do you ensure that there is a covering note which makes clear the copyright status of the item in order to remind users of their obligation to observe copyright law? Figure 10.2 is an example of a notice you can send with electronic products that are forwarded by e-mail.

Please be aware that we have paid the copyright fee for only one copy of this e-book/report/article. If you need another copy, let us know and we will order another copy and pay the appropriate copyright clearance fee. Please delete the electronic copy of the article after you have printed out a paper copy.

Figure 10.2 Sample copyright notice to attach when forwarding digital content

Each organization will have its own requirements for copying content, and will need to develop a policy which reflects those needs. In order to demonstrate that they are taking copyright seriously, there are a number of steps which can be taken.

10.4 Checklist of key things for keeping legal with copyright

Tip 1: If you need to consult the precise wording of copyright law, don't look at the Copyright, Designs and Patents Act 1988 as originally published, because there have been so many changes to the wording since then. Instead, you need to look for an annotated copy of the Act. These can be found in up-to-date legal textbooks (such as *Butterworths Intellectual Property Law Handbook*).

Tip 2: Look only for recent commentaries and books on copyright. They should be as current as possible, to take account of the many legislative changes which have taken place in recent years.

Tip 3: Think about whether you should have a notice on your library OPAC about document supply services. Figure 10.3 is a sample form of words relating specifically to the ordering of items through interlibrary loan.

Tip 4: Put copyright posters (see Chapter 10, section 10.1) next to photocopiers, scanners and computer terminals. Use the gold and blue posters or the CLA's copyright notices and excluded works list.

Tip 5: Do you undertake any copying which is not covered by the permitted acts/copyright exceptions? If so, you should consider taking out a licence to copy the material (e.g. with the Copyright Licensing Agency (www.cla.co.uk), the Newspaper Licensing Agency (www.nla.co.uk) or direct with the publisher).

Interlibrary loan requests
Are you requesting ILL photocopies for commercial purposes? Not sure? See the example scenarios set out in our copyright information notice. If yes, you need to use the copyright fee paid service. Ask a member of library staff before proceeding.

Figure 10.3 Copyright reminder for interlibrary loan photocopies

Tip 6: Make sure, if you are using copyright declaration forms, that they have the correct form of words on them. A model form of words for these can be found on the LACA website: www.cilip.org.uk/policyadvocacy/copyright/formsandposters/forms/forma.htm and www.cilip.org.uk/policyadvocacy/copyright/formsandposters/forms/formb.htm.

Tip 7: If you do not have any copyright licences for your organization and you wish to make copies which would be considered to be for a 'commercial purpose', make sure that they are 'legal' by purchasing copyright-cleared copies through a licensed document delivery service such as the British Library or under the CLA sticker scheme.

Tip 8: Develop standard copyright clearance forms for use when obtaining written permission to digitize material.

11

The copyright implications of freedom of information and the re-use of public sector information

11.1 Freedom of information

Public authorities complying with their statutory duty under sections 1 and 11 of the UK Freedom of Information Act 2000 to release information to an applicant are not breaching the Copyright, Designs and Patents Act 1988, according to guidance from what is now the Ministry of Justice (previously the Department for Constitutional Affairs). Chapter 8 of the procedural guidance on the Freedom of Information Act 2000 sets out the guidance on the interface between freedom of information and copyright (for the full guidance see www.dca.gov.uk/foi/guidance/proguide/chap08.htm):

 Use of Crown Copyright
Public authorities should be aware that information which is disclosed under the Act may be subject to copyright protection. If an applicant wishes to use any information in a way that would infringe copyright, for example by making multiple copies, or issuing copies to the public, he or she would require a licence from the copyright holder. HMSO have issued guidance on this subject in relation to Crown Copyright, which is available on HMSO's website, or by contacting HMSO at HMSO Licencing Division, St Clements House, 2-16 Colegate, Norwich, NR3 1BQ. Tel: 01613 621000, Fax: 01603 723000.

Third Party Copyright

Public authorities complying with their statutory duty under sections 1 and 11 of the Freedom of Information Act to release information to an applicant are not breaching the Copyright, Designs and Patents Act 1988. The FOIA specifically authorises release of the information to an applicant, even if it is in such a form as would otherwise breach the copyright interests of a third party. However, the Copyright, Designs and Patents Act 1988 will continue to protect the rights of the copyright holder once the information is received by the applicant.

The supply of information in response to a Freedom of Information request does not, therefore, grant the recipient an automatic right to re-use the material. The material is highly likely to be covered by copyright. That copyright may belong to the public sector information holder to whom the request has been made, but that is not necessarily the case. Under Freedom of Information legislation, a requester can ask for information *held* by a public authority, and this may be the copyright of someone else. Any re-use of material supplied in response to an FOI request would require the copyright owner's permission under UK law.

The further use by the recipient of any information supplied in response to an FOI request other than for the purposes of private study would count as re-use for which permission would be needed. In the UK this consent is often provided by the issuing of a licence which may be free or, in some cases, is subject to a charge. It is therefore recommended that responses to Freedom of Information requests should include a statement explaining the position as illustrated in Figure 11.1.

Copyright in information supplied under FOI

Most of the information that we provide in response to Freedom of Information Act 2000 requests will be subject to copyright protection. In most cases the copyright will be owned by [insert name of public sector authority]. The copyright in other information may be owned by another person or authority, as indicated by the information itself. You are free to use any information supplied for your own use. However, any other type of re-use, for example, by publishing the information on a website, will require the permission of the copyright holder.

Figure 11.1 Sample statement on copyright of material supplied under FOI

TIP: Unless you have permission from the rightsowner:
- Don't make further copies of information you receive in response to an FOI request.
- Don't post the contents of the response on your website.

Scotland

Scotland is covered by The Freedom of Information (Scotland) Act 2002 (Consequential Modifications) Order 2004: SI 2004/3089, www.opsi.gov.uk/si/si2004/ 20043089.htm.

Further information

OPSI Guidance Note 18, Information Asset Register and Freedom of Information – a co-ordinated response to information access, www.opsi.gov.uk/advice/crown-copyright/copyright-guidance/information-asset-register-and-freedom-of-information.htm.

OPSI Guidance Note 19, Freedom of Information Publication Schemes, www.opsi.gov.uk/advice/crown-copyright/copyright-guidance/freedom-of-information-publication-schemes.htm.

11.2 Environmental Information Regulations (EIR)

One of the exceptions to the duty to disclose environmental information relates to intellectual property. It appears as regulation 12(5)(c) in the UK Environmental Information Regulations 2004: SI 2004/3391, www.opsi.gov.uk/si/si2004/ 20043391.htm#12. The exception covers all copyright-protected material, patents and designs.

It is not the intention of the EIR to override and prejudice the rights of either an individual or a public authority. The issues involved are illustrated in the case study below.

CASE STUDY Ofcom v Information Commissioner

The Information Tribunal case of Ofcom v Information Commissioner[1] considered the exception relating to intellectual property under Regulation 12(5)(c) of the Environmental

Information Regulations. It involved a request for access to information about the location of mobile phone masts. The Tribunal concluded that the public interest in the release of the information was great enough to justify any damage to the intellectual property rights of the phone companies.

Ofcom and T-Mobile had said that the information requested formed part of a body of information which was protected by two categories of intellectual property right (namely copyright and database right).

The Information Tribunal decision acknowledges that once material protected by an intellectual property right has been released to a third party, it becomes more difficult to discover instances of infringement, to trace those responsible for it and to enforce the right against them.

The decision also considered whether the information was protected by the law of confidence. ■

Further information

Paragraphs 17–19 of the Code of Practice on the EIR,
    www.defra.gov.uk/corporate/opengov/eir/pdf/cop-eir.pdf.
www.ico.gov.uk/upload/documents/library/environmental_info_reg/
    introductory/introduction_to_eir_exceptions.pdf.
www.ico.gov.uk/upload/documents/library/freedom_of_information/
    detailed_specialist_guides/awareness_guidance_20_-
    _prejudice_and_adverse_affect.pdf.

11.3 Re-use of public sector information and copyright

The purpose of the Re-Use of Public Sector Information Regulations is not *access* to information – the Freedom of Information Act and other access legislation provide for that – but rather to provide a mechanism by which those seeking to *re-use* the information for a purpose other than that for which it was produced (for example, by publishing and making the information available to a wider audience) can obtain permission from those public authorities that control its use.

One of the important principles under the Regulations is that re-use of public sector information can only take place once access to information has been granted. A key point to note, therefore, is that any information that is exempt from release under FOI is not available for re-use. Or, to put it another way, any Freedom of Information application would have to be dealt with first, before re-use of the material could be allowed. Re-use cannot be granted unless access has been allowed.

The European Directive on the Re-use of Public Sector Information (2003/98/EC) was implemented in the UK through the Re-use of Public Sector Information Regulations 2005: SI 2005/1515. The regulations came into force on 1 July 2005 and they established a framework for making re-use easier and more transparent. The main obligations under the Re-Use of Public Sector Information Regulations 2005 are that:

- public sector documents that are available for re-use should be readily identifiable
- documents should generally be available for re-use at marginal cost
- public sector bodies should deal with applications to re-use information in a timely, open and transparent manner
- process should be fair, consistent and non-discriminatory
- sharing of best practice should be encouraged across the public sector.

The scheme to help make the re-use of public sector information both easy and transparent is overseen by the Office of Public Sector Information

---

- *Licence terms:* Public sector bodies have an obligation to publish licence terms whether in the form of a standard licence or a copyright notice on the material;
- *Details of charges:* where applicable these must be published and must be fair and consistent;
- *Responses to be within set time limits:* the time limit is 20 working days in line with Freedom of Information
- *Asset lists:* an obligation on public sector bodies to produce a list of material, both published and unpublished, which is available for re-use;
- *Robust complaints procedures:* Public sector bodies are required to publish details of their complaints process. In addition, a dispute resolution process has been implemented.

Figure 11.2 Main elements of the scheme for re-using public sector information (Source: www.opsi.gov.uk)

(OPSI) – which is part of The National Archives. Figure 11.2 shows the main elements of the scheme.

When considering what constitutes PSI, the re-use regulations refer to information as 'documents', which is defined as: 'any content, including any part of such content, whether in writing or stored in electronic form or as a sound, visual or audio-visual recording, other than a computer program' (see Regulation 4).

The scope of the regulations differs from the Freedom of Information regime. While FOI and the Re-use of Public Sector Information both relate to the public sector, nevertheless the range of public sector bodies covered by the two regimes does differ. Advice published on the OPSI website says:

 In the UK, the Regulations . . . cover most of the public sector. This includes:

- central government, including government trading funds and executive agencies;
- local government;
- the health service;
- Parliament.

There are, however, some notable exemptions. These are:

- public service broadcasters, such as the BBC;
- educational and research establishments, including schools and universities; and
- cultural organizations, such as museums, libraries and archives.

Further information

EC Directive 2003/98/EC on the Re-use of Public Sector Information, OJ (2003) L 354/90.

The Re-Use of Public Sector Information Regulations 2005: SI 2005/1515.

OPSI, www.opsi.gov.uk.

Advisory Panel on Public Sector Information, www.appsi.gov.uk/.

Note

1   Case number EA/2006/0010, www.informationtribunal.gov.uk/
     Documents/decisions/OFCOMvinfoComm_TMobile_4Aug07.pdf.

12

Developing a copyright policy

Organizations should act responsibly where copyright is concerned. Creating a culture of copyright compliance within your business will reduce the risk of copyright infringement.

Businesses should have a written policy for copyright compliance. It isn't appropriate to suggest a generic format for such a policy, because the corporate policy would need to be specific to the needs of the business and to reflect the range and types of copying that it undertakes.

If you have responsibility for copyright within your workplace, but your employer doesn't currently have a written policy on copyright, then I would advise you to work with senior management and your in-house lawyer – if there is one – to develop such a policy.

It may be that you do already have a number of statements which deal with copyright compliance, and that the problem you have is that they appear in a variety of different places, and that the statements aren't necessarily consistent with one another. There may, for example, be policy documents covering responsible use of company equipment and use of the internet or the company's intranet, but only a small part of these documents may relate specifically to copyright compliance. If this is the case, it is worth trying to bring together all of the different documents which mention copyright compliance and to ensure that they are consistent. There may be a number of people in different departments who each have a legitimate interest in monitoring and enforcing copyright compliance. The IT department may, for example, have a statement relating to the loading of software onto company equipment. One of its concerns will be to ensure that all the software used by the organization is properly licensed. The reprographics department may have written guidelines on how to ensure that any copying requested by staff complies with copyright legislation. The information service may have a statement about copyright compliance, or a set of FAQs on the topic. It will be concerned with observing copyright law, but staff will also need to ensure that the terms of any licence agreements for electronic products are properly observed.

Where you do have a range of policy statements which are produced by several different departments within the organization, it would be a good idea to have a designated person to field any queries about copyright. That way, staff don't have to worry about which department to contact, but instead have the 'copyright co-ordinator' as a central point of contact. If there is a need to liaise across several departments, the copyright co-ordinator can do that on behalf of staff and thereby ensure that the message being given out on copyright matters is consistent.

Making your organization copyright compliant isn't simply a question of drafting a policy, because any policy is worthless unless the staff are aware of and mindful of its contents; where any instance of a breach of policy occurs, it must be acted on. Figure 12.1 outlines the three key stages in developing a copyright policy.

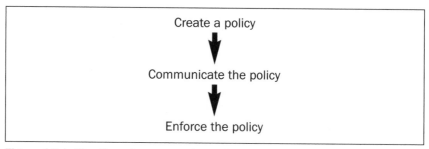

Figure 12.1 The three key stages in establishing a copyright policy

12.1 Creating a policy

There are two sides to creating a copyright compliance policy. On the one hand there is the question of protecting your own intellectual property, while on the other hand there is the matter of respecting the intellectual property rights of others. Both aspects should be covered within the policy statement.

The compliance policy should be tailored to the needs of your own organization. As such, consider for whom the policy is intended. For example does it address the issues relevant to both library staff and library users? What should it cover? What types of copying activities are undertaken regularly? What licences does the organization currently have, and what do they cover?

12.2 Communicating the policy

When you have reached the point of creating a formal copyright policy for your organization, the next stage is to decide the most effective way of communicating that policy. This is a crucial consideration if you are genuinely going to be able to achieve copyright compliance. Your company or institution's employees need to be aware of their obligations, and if they aren't then they should at least have a named contact to whom they can direct any copyright queries. Copyright law is complex, and you can't expect everyone to be a copyright expert. But you can make them aware of the potential risks, so that they get into the routine of checking with your key copyright contact rather than just going ahead and copying.

You then have to consider the most effective way of communicating the policy to staff. There will be some people who need to have a more in-depth knowledge of copyright issues than others – for example, if you have a reprographics department, a library or any department which is likely to regularly copy material – and this should be reflected in your communications strategy.

When debating the best way of getting the copyright compliance message across, you will need to think about such matters as:

- The document type(s) or format(s) to use: it may well be the case that it would be best to develop a number of different document types in order to reach different audiences. The policy could be summarized in a 'quick sheet', for example; a more detailed set of FAQs; and/or a more in-depth copyright policy statement.
- Whether the document is written in plain English: if it is full of

legal jargon, and requires a qualified lawyer to fully understand the wording of the document, people may not even bother trying to read it; or if they do, they may not understand it. Think carefully about the key messages that you need to get across – both in order to protect your own organization's content; and to ensure that you respect the intellectual property rights of others.

- Whether the policy document gives the details of who to contact as the central point for copyright queries. This should not be open to doubt.
- What methods should be used in order to communicate the policy: it might, for instance, be by e-mail, or by posting the policy statement on the organizational intranet. If, for example, you were to send an 'all staff' e-mail around the organization, directing them to a set of documentation about your copyright policy which you have posted on your intranet, how will new joiners be alerted to the policy?

12.3 Enforcing the policy

In order to enforce the copyright policy, an important pre-requisite is that you have got the support of your organization's top management. You will therefore need to take the time to explain to them why the policy is required, and draw to their attention the potential consequences of failing to have such a policy in place.

A co-ordinated approach is required. If you have many statements about copyright and other intellectual property rights issues in a number of different places, it will be important to ensure that they are consistent with one another. Equally, if you have a number of staff who have copyright responsibilities, you will need to make sure that they are all speaking with one voice.

If your organization has key departments where content is copied – for example a reprographics department or a library – it is important that their staff are confident that they understand the key points about respecting copyright.

If you have an acceptable use policy for your organization's IT equipment, for your network, or for your intranet, then those areas are key places to post a few essential points about copyright compliance.

Here are two examples of the content headings that you might include in a copyright guide.

Example 1 ABC University Copyright Guide

What is covered by copyright legislation?

Can I copy?

How long does copyright last?

Fair dealing for research or private study

Copying items from the internet

Copyright Licensing Agency

Newspaper Licensing Agency

Educational Recording Agency

British Standards

Ordnance Survey

Crown and parliamentary copyright

Theses and dissertations

Musical works

Video recordings

Open University programmes

Copyright in works generated by university staff and students

Example 2 Company XYZ's Copyright Guidelines

1 Copyright

1.1 What is copyright?

1.2 Duration of copyright

1.3 Who owns copyright?

1.4 Photographs

1.5 Copyright licensing

1.6 Crown copyright

2 Infringement of copyright

2.1 What is infringement?

2.2 Computer programs

2.3 The internet

2.4 The NLA and CLA

2.5 Secondary infringement

3 What are you allowed to copy?

3.1 Authorized reproduction

Appendix
Sample clauses for inclusion in a copyright policy

- Unauthorized copying of a third party's work, including making a hard copy or electronic copy or simply storing the work without the permission of the owner, may constitute copyright infringement. You are not entitled to make unlimited use of copyright-protected works which are accessible on the internet, intranet or other organizational systems. Copying third party property may expose both the organization and yourself to actions for infringement, including claims for damages.
- Do not use a third party's brand or business name without prior permission. Do not take unfair advantage or use them in a manner which is detrimental to the character or reputation of that brand or name.
- Do not reproduce copyrighted material without the authorization of the copyright owner.
- You may copy from a literary, dramatic, musical or artistic work (but not a film or sound recording) for your own interest or private study where this is for a non-commercial purpose, but you cannot reproduce that copy for others. Unless it is impracticable to do so, all copies that are made must be properly acknowledged.
- You may reproduce limited excerpts from a work for the purpose of criticism, review or news reporting. Unless it is impracticable to do so, all copies that are made must be properly acknowledged.
- Organizational content appearing on or available through the intranet

may also be of a confidential or otherwise sensitive nature. Therefore you should not provide copies of the content or otherwise make it available to any person who is not authorized to access it directly on this site unless you first obtain appropriate authorization.

- [The copyright policy document should name a contact within the organization who can act as the first point of contact for any queries about copyright law or the organization's copyright policy.]

Further information

Blackstone's Statutes on Intellectual Property, 8th edn, Andrew Christie and
Stephen Gare (eds), Oxford University Press, 2006, ISBN 978-0199288267.
Butterworths Intellectual Property Law Handbook, Jeremy Philipps (ed.), 8th rev.
edn, 2007, ISBN 978-1405715850.
Case Western Reserve University, Copyright compliance policy,
http://library.case.edu/copyright.
Copywatch, www.copywatch.org (CLA's copyright compliance website).
Ethical principles and code of professional practice for library and information
professionals, CILIP, www.cilip.org.uk/policyadvocacy/ethics.
Grossman, Wendy (2007) A Picture Paints a Thousand Invoices, *Guardian*, 1
February, www.guardian.co.uk/technology/2007/feb/01/copyright.newmedia.
Infoethics – CILIP Information Ethics website,
www.infoethics.org.uk/CILIP/admin/index.htm.
Jassin, Lloyd, and Schechter, Steven (1998) *The Copyright Permission and Libel
Handbook*, Wiley, ISBN 978-0-471-14654-4.
Norman, Sandy (2004) *Practical Copyright for Information Professionals: the
CILIP handbook*, Facet Publishing, ISBN 978-1-85604-490-5.

Stim, Richard (1999) *Getting Permission: how to license and clear copyrighted materials online and off,* Nolo Press.

HM Treasury (2006) *Gowers Review of Intellectual Property,* HMSO, ISBN 9-780118-4083-9.

Table F.1 Where to go to seek advice

Organization	E-mail/website
CILIP's information and advisory service	info@cilip.org.uk (CILIP members only)
Libraries and Archives Copyright Alliance	www.cilip.org.uk/laca LACA lobbies the government and the EU on all aspects of copyright on behalf of UK libraries, archives and information services and their users.
IPR Helpdesk	www.ipr-helpdesk.org
JISC Legal	www.jisclegal.ac.uk Serves the higher and further education communities.

Index